LOST R₄
OF LEICES
& RUTLAND

Other areas covered in our
Lost Railways series include:

Berkshire

Cheshire

Chilterns

Dorset

East Anglia

Hampshire

Herefordshire & Worcesteshire

Kent

Lancashire

Merseyside & Greater Manchester

Middlesex

Northumberland

Nottinghamshire

Shropshire

Staffordshire

Surrey

Sussex

Wiltshire

North & East Yorkshire

LOST RAILWAYS
OF LEICESTERSHIRE
& RUTLAND

Geoffrey Kingscott

COUNTRYSIDE BOOKS
NEWBURY, BERKSHIRE

First published 2006
© Geoffrey Kingscott 2006

COUNTRYSIDE BOOKS
3 Catherine Road
Newbury, Berkshire

To view our complete range of books,
please visit us at
www.countrysidebooks.co.uk

ISBN 1 85306 991 4
EAN 978 1 85306 991 8

The cover picture shows a BR Standard
4-6-0 4MT class No 75059 passing
Knighton South junction signalbox and is
from an original painting by Colin Doggett

Produced through MRM Associates Ltd., Reading
Typeset by Mac Style, Nafferton, E. Yorkshire
Printed by Woolnough Bookbinding Ltd., Irthlingborough

CONTENTS

ABBREVIATIONS

The following abbreviations are used in this book:

ANJR	Ashby & Nuneaton Joint Railway
BR	British Railways
CFR	Charnwood Forest Railway
GCR	Great Central Railway
GNR	Great Northern Railway
LMSR	London, Midland & Scottish Railway
L&NER	London & North Eastern Railway
L&NWR	London & North Western Railway
L&SR	London & Swannington Railway
MR	Midland Railway

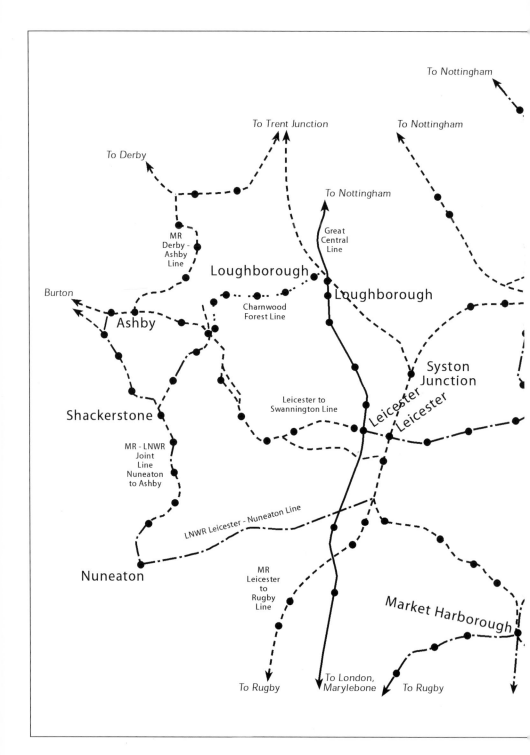

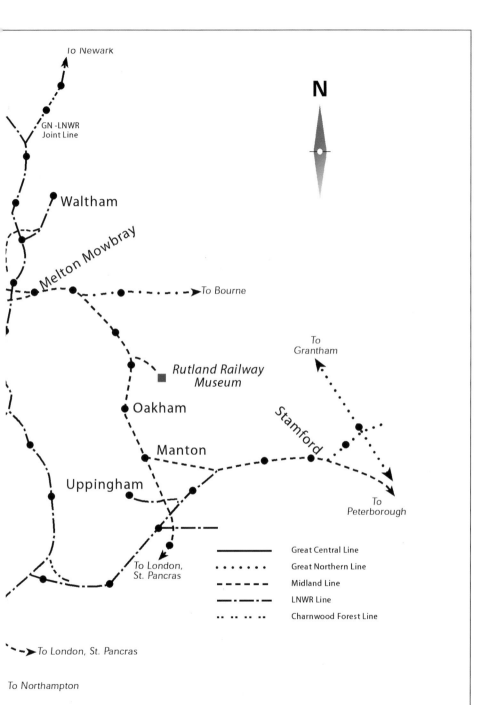

Introduction

Station Hill, Station Close, Station Mews, Station Avenue, Station Farm, Station Cottages, Station Hollow, Station Lane, Station Street, Station Terrace – these names occur frequently in Leicestershire. This is not to mention the 55 Station Roads which can be found in the county. Each and every one indicates that a passenger railway once passed nearby.

For the most part, the trains no longer run, and the rails have been taken up. However, it is surprising just how many of the trackbeds are still there, overgrown perhaps and inaccessible, but still clearly to be seen tracing their line across the fields. Where the lines cross over roads, the bridges have usually been removed, but not always.

In short, there is a lot to be seen in Leicestershire of the county's lost railways, if you know where to look.

By 'lost railway' I have taken, as a definition, a railway which once carried passenger traffic, and does so no more. This means that the Leicester & Swannington Railway, which is covered in chapter 1, can be included, since although parts of it still carry freight, it is no longer used for passenger services. However, it excludes a route such as the main Derby to London line, since this is still used, with stations at Loughborough and Leicester, even though many of the smaller stations, such as Kegworth, have been closed.

Railway travel reached its peak in the Edwardian era, and Leicestershire was no exception. There were then 75 stations in the county, every one manned with a full complement of staff, serving a complex web of main lines and branch lines. Today only ten of these survive as stations on the main railway network, and some of these have been reduced to the status of unmanned halts. More happily, however, another five survive on heritage railway lines.

A visit to the restored Quorn station will show just what a self-sufficient entity a little village station could provide, with its booking office and waiting rooms. In the present age, when we think nothing of flying off to the Seychelles for a holiday, or jumping in the car and driving to Devon, it is difficult to imagine the Victorian mindset. But just a century ago the local railway station was the only outlet to the world beyond the village. Everyone, from landowner to farm labourer, used it and bought tickets at the same booking office window whenever they wanted to travel more than a few miles from home.

Four major companies from the pre-1923 railway grouping were active in Leicestershire – the Midland Railway (MR), the London & North Western (LNWR), the Great Northern (GNR) and the Great Central (GCR). Grouping, which took place on 1 January 1923, was a process which brought over a hundred independent railway companies into four main groups: London Midland and Scottish Railway (LMS), London & North Eastern Railway (LNER), Great Western Railway (GWR) and Southern Railway (SR). The LMS and LNER were both active in Leicestershire, the former taking over the MR and the LNWR, and the latter the GNR and the GCR.

The development of railways in Leicestershire was much influenced by the county's geography.

The north-south route (Loughborough – Leicester – Market Harborough) was the easy one, with the valley of the River Soar from the northern boundary of the county

11

down to the city of Leicester, and the valley of the River Sence to the south, providing a low level obvious route. Even today, Loughborough, Leicester and Market Harborough remain the three most important railway towns in the county. The Midland Railway came this way. Later, the Great Central also came via Loughborough and Leicester, its lines criss-crossing the Midland's twice, but then preferred to go via Lutterworth rather than Market Harborough.

The valley of the Trent, to the north of the county, and the valley of the Welland to the south, do provide some east-west routes, but much of Leicestershire consists of hills. In the east, the Leicestershire Wolds are quite sparsely populated and, while the GNR-LNWR Bottesford Junction

Staff outside Market Harborough station in 1885. (Market Harborough Museum)

to Hallaton line was a magnificent piece of engineering, and passed through attractive countryside, it had little chance of paying its way once alternative forms of transport were available. To the west of Leicester lie the Charnwood Forest hills, but this area is rich in coal and minerals, and parts of it have been industrial from time immemorial.

So far I have only mentioned lines in Leicestershire. The county of Rutland is dealt with in a separate chapter, as is its right. With the possible exception of Yorkshiremen there are no local residents more proud of their county than Rutlanders. They always emphasise that they are not an appendage of Leicestershire, and indeed their county is bigger than you might think. The Midland Railway's Syston to Peterborough line bisects Rutland, with a station in the county town of Oakham. A branch, from Manton Junction to Kettering, now freight only, crosses one of the great railway sights of the Midlands, the 82-arch Harringworth viaduct, the longest rural viaduct in England.

Each expedition I undertook to find old railways was preceded by a planning session. My companions and I relied heavily on the Ordnance Survey Explorer 1:25,000 scale series of maps. Those numbered 222, 232, 233, 234, 245 and 246 cover Leicestershire and Rutland, and clearly show where there are traces of a 'Dismantled Railway'. The Ordnance Survey also now offer for sale their old maps, and we purchased their 1905 one-inch to a mile series for the two counties. These show the railway network at its peak, and are particularly valuable for pinpointing the location of lost rural stations.

One advantage we enjoyed was that modern footpaths are usually clearly marked in Leicestershire, which has an excellent reputation in this respect. I had an illuminating interview with Bill Carter, Rights of Way manager for the county. He confirmed there was no formal policy for using old railway trackbeds as footpaths, but cases for improvement are assessed on merit.

A good example of a trackbed which became a path (and bridleway) is the Glenfield to Ratby section of the Leicester-Swannington line (see chapter 1). After the trackbed became disused for railway purposes, people started using it as an informal path. Eventually the parish council made an application for this to be formally registered as a definite right of way, which was successful, and the land was then purchased from the owner.

This book uses Imperial measurements such as the yard (0.9 metres) and the mile (1.6 km). One unit of measure which was common in railway use but which is much less familiar these days is the chain. Early surveyors used a physical chain, made up of a series of linked measuring rods, when they were checking out linear distances, and railway lengths such as those of lines or tunnels were often quoted in chains. A chain is 22 yards, and is easy to visualise, for it is exactly the length of a cricket pitch, from one wicket to the other. Ordnance Survey grid references (eg SK 383190) are also given to locate particular features. Instructions on how to interpret these are on each OS map.

Where the line once taken by Leicestershire's old railways is still accessible, I have walked the route, usually in the company of my brother-in-law Rodger Smith (who took most of the photographic record) and my younger son, Laurence. Sometimes we have stretched the meaning of the word 'accessible'; it might mean slithering down an embankment, or forcing our way through bramble and hawthorn. We have never knowingly trespassed, but it must be emphasised that because a scene is photographed or described in this book it does not mean there is an automatic right of way or right of access.

My two companions accompanied me for little reward except for a liquid one. Earlier I mentioned the number of Station Roads or Station Streets we came across in Leicestershire and Rutland. Another indication of the importance the railways once had for the communities they served is the names of public houses – Station Hotel, Midland Hotel, Railway Inn. In the interests of research, I and my fellow investigators have done our best to have a drink in every Leicestershire pub bearing a railway-related name!

Apart from my son and brother-in-law, I also have to thank the many individuals who helped with anecdotes or pointed us in the direction of further research. Library or museum staff at Leicester, Ashby-de-la-Zouch and Loughborough have always been willing to assist. But perhaps the most rewarding were the conversations we had with local people when we were checking out the sites of the old railways – everyone, without exception, remembered the railways with nostalgic affection, and many expressed the wish that their local line be reopened. So perhaps some of the lost railways will not be lost forever!

Geoffrey Kingscott

1
First in the East Midlands

The Leicester & Swannington Railway

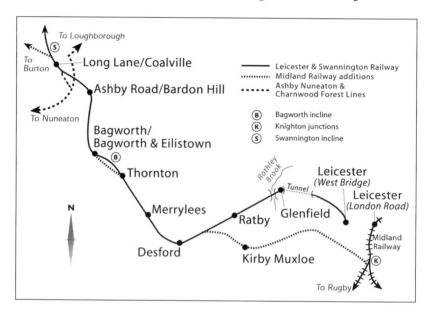

Leicester wanted coal. It wanted lots of coal. The city had been a traditional centre for making worsted stockings and knitted goods for a long time but by the 1770s the advances of the Industrial Revolution meant that textile goods of this kind could be made by machine. But coal was needed to heat the new factories and the homes of the workers who flocked to Leicester to work in them. Then, as engineers mastered steam power, coal was also needed to power the machinery.

To the north-west of the city lay several rich coal seams. These had been worked in a minor way for some six centuries, but unfortunately the Charnwood Hills lay between the coalfields and the city, and transporting that coal, at first by pack-mule and then, as road surfaces gradually improved, by cart, was slow and expensive. Demand soon started to outstrip supply.

In 1779 a different method of transport – the canal – changed the economics of the situation. With the opening of the Erewash Canal and the River Soar Navigation, coal could be brought by boat right into the centre of Leicester. To the fury of the Leicestershire coal-owners, coal in plenty from the Derbyshire and Nottinghamshire Erewash Valley coalfield, over 30 miles away, could be sold much more cheaply than that from the nearby Charnwood Forest workings.

The Leicestershire coal-owners tried to find ways of competing. They did manage to construct the nine-mile long Charnwood Forest Canal, which led to a tramway down to the Loughborough Navigation, part of the Soar system. Haulage from the collieries to the canal at its upper end at Thringstone Bridge was also by short horse-operated tramways. Unfortunately, in 1799, severe weather destroyed the Blackbrook reservoir (which supplied water to the canal) and damaged the canal embankments beyond repair. For another 30 years, the Erewash Valley coal-owners continued to enjoy their price advantage over Leicestershire coal.

Then, William Stenson, who was part owner of the Long Lane pit near Whitwick, heard about something quite new happening in the north of England – a long-distance railway line using not just horses but also a new invention: the steam locomotive.

Now William Stenson must have been very well-informed, since the railway revolution had hardly started. It is believed that Stenson even visited the world's first public railway, the Stockton & Darlington, in its very first year of operation, in 1828.

And it was in 1828 that he and his fellow coal-owners applied to the company which controlled the now disused Charnwood Forest Canal. The idea was to lay rails along the dry canal bed, to bring coal from Whitwick and Swannington to Loughborough, where it could then be transferred onto boats, and brought into Leicester at West Bridge wharf. This was turned down, but Stenson, who was also something of a surveyor, went out with his theodolite (an instrument for measuring horizontal and verticle angles), and plotted a new route. In a letter to his friend John Ellis, an influential Leicester businessman, he wrote: 'Our carting beats us, but I see a way of relief if we can but get up a railway company. I've tried the ground with my theodolite and find no difficulty in making, though a tunnel will have to be made through the hill at Glenfield and further there will have to be a severe incline near to Bagworth.'

He and Ellis brought together the Leicestershire coal-owners at the Bell Hotel in the Humberstone Gate area of Leicester. The result of their deliberations was the complete 1829 proposal for the Leicester and Swannington Railway (LSR), and this was turned into a parliamentary bill the same year. It became an Act of Parliament in 1830, only the fifth railway bill to go through and the first of its kind in the Midlands. Indeed, the Act was passed two and a half months before the opening of the Liverpool & Manchester Railway, which is generally reckoned as the key event that ushered in the railway age.

Obviously, with few precedents to guide them, the Leicestershire coal-owners needed expert help. So John Ellis went off to see the one man who knew about railways, George Stephenson himself. George, with his son Robert, was persuaded to dine with Ellis and look at Stenson's maps. As a result George and Robert came to Leicester and Robert, then aged only 27, was appointed engineer in charge of the new railway. George and Robert also took shares in the company.

Before the rails were laid, George Stephenson was consulted as to which gauge should be used. He

A picture of the Comet *locomotive coming out of the Glenfield tunnel is included in this mural at Stephenson Drive, Leicester, overlooking a surviving part of the trackbed. (Rodger Smith)*

recommended what is now the standard gauge (4 ft 8½ inches). At the same time, he was also advising on the construction of the Canterbury & Whitstable Railway in Kent, and recommended the same gauge. With a foresight unusual for the time, he commented: 'Make them of the same width; though they may be a long way apart now, depend upon it, they will be joined together some day.'

Work started towards the end of 1830. There was a temporary hitch when, in 1831, the contractor for the Glenfield tunnel, Daniel Jowitt, fell down a tunnel shaft and died from his injuries, but the Leicester & Swannington Railway opened on 17 July 1832. Initially it ran for eleven miles, from Leicester West Bridge to Bagworth Staunton Road.

On that July day church bells were rung, gun salutes were fired, and there was wining and dining. The first train was pulled by the locomotive *Comet*, brought from Newcastle by sea and canal, and driven by George Stephenson himself, assisted by his son Robert and a local man, Robert Weatherburn, who was to become the regular driver.

The train consisted of new, open coal trucks, across which planks of wood were laid as seats, and the distinguished guests cheerfully took their places in this extemporised accommodation. All went well until the train was in the darkness of the Glenfield tunnel, where the chimney of the *Comet* struck the roof and was knocked off. The train came to a halt. Smoke billowed back through the tunnel, but there seems to have been no panic – as none of the passengers had ever been on a train before, perhaps they thought it was all quite normal. When the engine got under way again, however, and they emerged from the tunnel, there was considerable dismay when everyone

The Rothley Brook (also known as the Glenfield Brook) where it is crossed by the railway. (Rodger Smith)

found they had blackened faces and blackened clothes. The train therefore stopped where the line crossed the Rothley Brook, and most of the party got down and washed their faces in the stream, using their pocket handkerchiefs as towels. The rest of the journey passed without further mishap.

The 'Upper Level' stretch of line from Bagworth to Ashby Road (later renamed Bardon Hill) opened in February 1833. The line to Long Lane (later renamed Coalville) was opened for freight on 22 April, 1883 and, five days later, passengers could travel between Leicester and Coalville. The last stretch of the line, from Coalville to the foot of the Swannington incline, was completed on 25 November 1833.

Trains from Leicester – usually consisting of empty coal wagons – ran to Bagworth station, where the locomotive was detached. The empty wagons were then connected to a rope. Loaded wagons brought by another locomotive to the top of the 1 in 29 incline were lowered down, their weight pulling the empty wagons up. Passengers could apparently choose whether to walk up the incline or take the risk of riding up in one of the empty wagons. Eventually, in 1848, the incline was by-passed by a two-mile deviation of the line.

George Stephenson, though a largely uneducated man, did have a shrewd business brain. During the excavations to build the LSR, his son Robert had noticed rich coal seams at Snibston, not yet tapped. With his Liverpool financier friends, George bought himself a large estate nearby and started to dig for coal. In 1831, to keep a closer eye on his investments, he moved to Alton Grange, near Ashby-de-la-Zouch, and this was his residence for several years. Not that he was there very much, for the 1830s were his busiest period. Because he wanted to keep the direction of as much railway development in his own hands as possible, he was soon travelling not only in the UK but in Europe as well.

The population in and around the coalfield grew, and it was in 1847 that the hamlet of Long Lane, now a bustling township, was formally given the new name of Coalville.

The Leicester & Swannington railway fulfilled all the aspirations of the Charnwood Forest coal-owners, and Leicestershire coal, now cheaper than its Erewash Valley competitor, poured into Leicester. The only losers were the Erewash Valley coal-owners, who at first tried to get the canal companies to lower their charges. When this failed, they decided to build their own railway. This project took on a life of its own, and became the Midland Counties Railway (although the Erewash Valley line itself was not to be built for another ten years). The Midland Counties Railway was one of the three companies which merged in 1844 to become the Midland Railway.

And, in 1847, the Midland Railway, already becoming a force in national railway politics thanks to its thrusting chairman, George Hudson ('The Railway King', as he became known), acquired the Leicester & Swannington. The LSR had used as its emblem a mythical beast called the wyvern, which had been emblazoned on the standards of the rulers of Mercia, the ancient Midlands kingdom. The Midland Railway took over the wyvern device as its own.

The LSR's man, John Ellis, joined the board and after George Hudson had become discredited through over-speculation, it was the honest Leicester Quaker John Ellis who became chairman of the Midland Railway.

As the purpose of the Leicester & Swannington was specifically to bring coal to Leicester, the railway company showed little interest in passengers. They could be carried, but in an open carriage called a tub with standing accommodation only. Tickets were in the form of brass tokens. Not long after the opening of the line, however, bowing to demand, they did produce a first-class carriage, but mixed passenger and freight trains were still the norm until as late as 1888.

The site selected for the Leicester terminus at West Bridge was on the flat water meadows on the western banks of the River Soar, which gave ample room for sidings and coal wharves. The first platform at West Bridge

This mock-up has been created on the exact site of the old West Bridge station, a valuable reminder that the first steam railway ever built in the East Midlands started from here. (Rodger Smith)

was provided in 1876, and a formal station was opened on 13 March 1893, at the southern end of the site.

Because the line was mainly used for coal trains, the locomotives were powerful ones for that era and were given appropriately heroic names. The first ten engines were called *Comet, Phoenix, Samson, Goliath, Hercules, Atlas, Liverpool, Vulcan, Ajax* and *Hector*. The original 13 ft chimney of *Comet* was reduced in height after the Glenfield tunnel accident.

From West Bridge the railway climbed out of Leicester in a north-westerly direction, and up to Glenfield Hill, a ridge

24

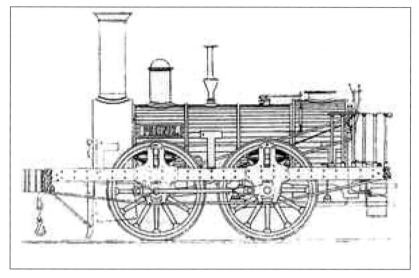

A drawing of the Phoenix, *one of the early locomotives on the line. (By permission of Railtrack)*

of sand and clay, and the Glenfield tunnel. These were early days in railway building, and this tunnel was narrower and lower than what was later to become standard railway practice. This meant that throughout its life only special rolling stock could be used. Its length was 1,796 yards (ie 36 yards more than a mile), an extraordinary achievement for the time. It was completely straight, and almost level but without any wall refuges.

The section of the line between West Bridge and Desford diminished in importance after 1 August 1849, when the Midland Railway completed a link between Knighton Junction and Desford, thereby incorporating the Leicester & Swannington into the main railway network. The last passenger service between West Bridge and Desford ran on 22 September 1928, but freight continued until April 1966.

The tunnel, which today runs under housing between Stephenson Court (appropriate name) and Copeland Avenue in Leicester, was finally sealed in 1969. It is owned and maintained by the Leicester Corporation, who would sell it if they could find someone to take on the heavy responsibility. There are five ventilation shafts, all Grade II listed. The tunnel actually runs under the city boundary of Leicester and into the district of Blaby, which has incorporated the tunnel entrance into its coat of arms.

This plaque in the grounds of a housing complex marks the site of Glenfield station. (Rodger Smith)

The station at Glenfield, after the tunnel, has long since disappeared, and warden-controlled housing now covers the site. However, a plaque in the grounds marks where the station once stood. Nearby, on the opposite side of the road, is a Railway Hotel.

Opposite the site of Glenfield station there is a footpath and cycle path to Ratby, and this follows the route of the old railway. This path is variously known as Comet Way, Rocket Way or Stephenson Way. A short walk along it brings you to the bridge crossing the Rothley Brook and the spot where the soot-blackened passengers washed themselves as best they could after the Glenfield tunnel incident on that memorable first journey over 160 years ago.

The Railway Inn, Ratby, today. (Rodger Smith)

27

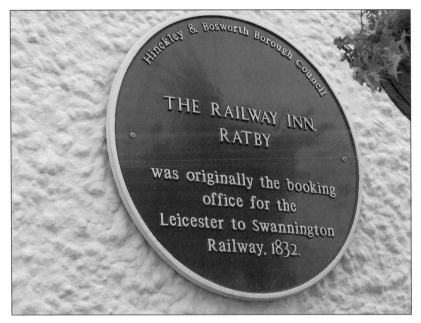

The inn's use as the first booking office is recorded by this plaque. (Rodger Smith)

Another commemorative memorial, built from wooden railway sleepers, can be found at the Ratby end of the path. Ratby station was opened in 1873. It was originally just a halt, with a public house (later renamed the Railway Inn) serving as the booking office. A blue plaque on the wall commemorates this, and inside the railway theme is continued with pictures on the walls, including one of the inn as it looked in the 19th century.

Desford station was some distance from its village. Desford was not only on the original line through Glenfield tunnel but also on the Midland Railway line from Knighton Junction. The station closed on 7 September

Part of the winding gear left behind at the Swannington Incline. (Judy Wheldon)

1964, and the building is now a private house. Going back down the Knighton link, the only intermediate station between Desford and Leicester was Kirkby Muxloe, which closed the same day.

Shortly before Bagworth the railway crossed Thornton Lane, where an inn known as the Stag and Castle (the building still survives) once issued railway tickets. This was abandoned as a halt in 1841, but the cinder path in front of it marks the former trackbed.

This spot is famous in railway history, as giving rise to the origin of the steam whistle. On 4 May 1833, a collision is said to have occurred (there are no documentary records of the accident) between the locomotive *Samson* and a farm cart

29

The winding engine, technically advanced for its time, used on the Swannington Incline. It has been restored and is now in the National Railway Museum at York. (Judy Wheldon)

carrying beetroot and eggs to Leicester market. Up to this time the usual locomotive warning device was a horn, as with horse-driven coaches, but it was found to be ineffective over the noise of the engine. As a result efforts were made to produce something better, and the steam whistle was invented by a musical instrument manufacturer working to suggestions made by George Stephenson. Whistles shortly afterwards became compulsory for all locomotives.

The line from Leicester went to the Swannington Incline. The incline site is now preserved. The winding engine at the top of the incline operated satisfactorily for a century, at first winding up coal wagons from collieries to the early railway, then later winding coal wagons down in order to fuel engines pumping water out of the collieries after they became disused. This engine, built to the specifications of Robert Stephenson, was an example of an early use of a piston valve. It was made by the Horsley Iron & Coal Co and, with subsequent improvements, continued to operate until 1947, when it was replaced by electric pumps. It is now at the National Railway Museum in York.

Following the acquisition of the Leicester & Swannington line by the Midland Railway, it was integrated into the growing national rail network. This was when the connection was made from Desford to Knighton Junction, bypassing the Glenfield section. At the same time the deviation was created through Thornton to avoid the Bagworth self-acting incline. The deviation still required a gradient of 1 in 66 to be climbed, but this was possible for the locomotives of 1847, now much more powerful than the pioneer engines of 1832. After 1847 the line became part of a through route between Leicester and Burton, and was made double track throughout its length, except for the Glenfield section.

2
Lines round
Ashby-de-la-Zouch

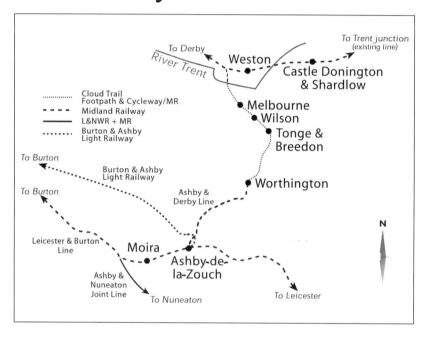

Today, Ashby-de-la-Zouch is the most important town in Leicestershire not to have a railway passenger service, despite its 19th century status as a meeting place for different lines.

First came the extension to the Leicester & Swannington Railway. When they bought this already profitable company in 1846, the Midland Railway immediately set about extending it through Ashby-de-la-Zouch to

Burton-on-Trent. They constructed a new line from a junction north of Coalville station. This continued to the south of Ashby, which was then developing as a spa town, with some ambitious hotel development.

Ashby-de-la-Zouch station, opened on 1 August 1849, was built to enhance the town's claim to elegance. The building is in an unusual Grecian style, with the main entrance flanked by Doric columns, reflecting a similar style used for the Ivanhoe Baths (since demolished) and what is now the Royal Hotel. The station and its forecourt still exist, though the building is today used as private offices.

After Ashby, before the line left the county and entered Derbyshire on its way to Staffordshire's Burton-on-Trent, there was one more station in Leicestershire. This was at Moira. The station building is still there (access via Station Drive, off Ashby Road), boarded up and suffering from some vandalism. Its basic structure and decorative features are, however, intact and it is crying out for renovation. This station once had sidings, and their site can still be seen. Near the entrance to Station Drive is one of Leicestershire's many Railway inns.

The line was closed to passenger traffic on 7 September 1964, when Ashby and Moira stations were closed. Heavy freight continues to use the line infrequently but there is much talk of reopening it again one day as the Ivanhoe Line or the National Forest Line.

Let us now return to Ashby station where, in the station forecourt, set in the cobbles, there is still to be seen a short length of tramway track. For Ashby was the terminus of the Burton & Ashby Light Railway, a 3 ft 6 in gauge tramway built and operated by the Midland Railway, primarily to keep out competition. It ran from 1906 to 1927,

The boarded up Moira station today. (Rodger Smith)

with open-top trams, and went via the colliery towns of Woodville, Swadlincote and Newhall, terminating just beyond the Midland Railway's station in Burton-on-Trent. Between Ashby and Woodville the track is still there, buried about ten to twelve inches below the modern road surface. One of its tramcars was salvaged and, curiously, is now located in Detroit, USA.

One further railway line out of Ashby, now completely lost to rail traffic, connected Ashby and Derby via Melbourne, a more direct route than the one via Burton.

In 1846 the Midland Railway had acquired the Ashby Canal and its ancillary colliery and limestone tramways. One of these was the Ticknall tramway, built in 1802 so that

The Railway inn at Moira. (Rodger Smith)

horses could pull loads from the brickyards north of Ticknall and limeyards south of it to a junction with the canal at Willersley. A bridge which took the tramway over the road in the village of Ticknall itself, and which is still intact, is one of the oldest railway bridges in the world.

The Midland Railway decided to rebuild the section between Cloud Hill quarry (near Worthington) and Ashby as a standard-gauge railway, and constructed a new line from Cloud Hill to Pear Tree (Derby) where it linked up with an existing line. In January 1874 it became a passenger service between Ashby and Derby but survived only until 1930. The line itself kept going until 1981, with freight traffic from the quarries along the route.

Derby-bound passenger trains left Ashby from the same station as the Leicester-Burton trains, but from a platform

The Ticknall tramway arch, still spanning the main road at Ticknall. Dating from 1802, it is one of the oldest railway bridges in the world. (Rodger Smith)

that was set apart from the grandiose main buildings, and built at a different angle. This meant that the Ashby station complex was quite extensive. Today, if you follow Pithiviers Close to its end and look over a fence, you can see where the track started to branch for the Derby line, with the stone building of the former station a considerable distance behind you. There are some bungalows here, and a decorative feature on the lawns seems to include stone suspiciously like old platform edging, round a tree. The Derby platform would have ended in what is now the yard of the fire station, as is evident from a line of trees that can be seen on old photographs.

This pre-First World War picture shows trams in the forecourt of Ashby station. The occasion was said to be a Board of Trade inspection, but the photographer had evidently got a group of children and adults in their best clothes to pose for the picture. (Ashby-de-la-Zouch Museum)

A path between Wilfred Place and Kilwardby Street, called Churchside Walk, and an adjoining service road to new housing follow the alignment of the old railway. One of the modern houses here has been given the name of Railway Cuttings, with an engraving of a locomotive. The Fallen Knight hotel at the end of the path, on the other side of Kilwardby Street, was formerly the Midland Hotel. Another street, Trinity Court, is on the alignment. Opposite the entrance to Trinity Court you can see a gate on the site of an old level-crossing. The original crossing-keeper's house, its windows looking on to where the railway passed rather than on to the road, is still there. If

Ashby-de-la-Zouch. *Midland Railway Station.*

The elegance of the classical exterior of Ashby-de-la-Zouch station was not matched by its platforms, with these rather ugly canopies. (Ashby-de-la-Zouch Museum)

Another picture taken in Ashby station forecourt, showing a side view of the tram and, behind the small boy, a sign pointing to the goods stations.

Ashby station buildings today. They are used as private offices. Note the tram rails in the foreground. (Rodger Smith)

you look over the gate into the field, the main alignment goes straight ahead, and a branch to a soap factory (the original tramway route) curves away to the right. To the left is a siding to the old mill buildings.

On the branch, at the site of Callis Bridge, there is new housing called Bridge Place. Callis Bridge carried the tramway over the road, the branch itself deviating from the line of the tramway at this point. The abutment can be seen but the bridge was demolished on 1 January 1969, according to a commemorative plaque at this spot.

Off Smisby Road three streets, all cul-de-sacs – Holywell Avenue, King George Avenue and Clifton Avenue – all end where the railway used to run.

Laying the rails during the building of the Ashby to Derby line. (Ashby-de-la-Zouch Museum)

After leaving Ashby there are only occasional traces of the line as it headed north-east through Old Parks tunnel to Lount Wood. The Ivanhoe Way, Leicestershire's popular long-distance footpath, crosses the route but there is nothing to be seen. A few yards forward from a lay-by on the B587 road near Lount (SK 383190) are some metal railings, where the railway used to pass under the road. The line of the trackbed can be made out from the break in the trees, but new trees have been planted on the trackbed itself (this area is part of the National Forest) and soon this trace will also be lost.

Looking at the Derby to Ashby line from a different direction to that described in the text, where it ran through the middle of Ashby town, with the mill siding in the foreground and the soap factory branch coming in from the left. (Ashby-de-la-Zouch Museum)

All the intermediate stations on the line were simple structures. The first was a halt at Worthington, opened 1 January 1864 but little used by passengers up to its

The Cloud Trail cycleway passing the much-altered Tonge & Breedon station. The buildings now form part of a private house.

closure on 22 September 1930. However, there were a number of industrial sidings at this point.

After Worthington, practically the whole route as far as Swarkestone in Derbyshire has been preserved and turned into the Cloud Trail, a 13-mile walking and cycling path. You can follow the Trail from the car park in Worthington (SK 210405). After about a mile you come to gates, where care has to be taken on some days because monster vehicles carrying quarry material are constantly passing. Not far after that comes the one break in the line, where the former trackbed has been sliced through by the busy A42 dual-carriageway road. From the diversion necessitated by this, Breedon church in its dramatic situation on an

Although the line through Coalville no longer carried passenger traffic, in British Rail days a series of highly successful open days was held at the Marton Lane depot in Coalville. Here, three trainspotters gaze at the powerful lines of a diesel locomotive in 1985. (Leicester Mercury)

On the occasion of a special VIP train being run on the line through Ellistown in 1986, a group of miners from Ellistown Colliery staged a demonstration suggesting re-opening the line to passenger traffic. (Leicester Mercury)

43

The magnificent bridge by which the Ashby to Derby line, now the Cloud Trail, crosses the River Trent. (Rodger Smith)

isolated hill comes suddenly into view. This church is the oldest known Christian site in the East Midlands.

After passing through a deep cutting below the tiny village of Tonge there is a long straight stretch and just after the B587 road is the site of Tonge & Breedon station. The station buildings, much altered, are now part of a private house.

When the line opened there was also a station at Wilson, a tiny hamlet just inside the Leicestershire county boundary, before the track entered Derbyshire. Wilson's population (according to the 1871 census) was only 144. Wilson station therefore closed after only two years and a house was built on the site.

This ends the Leicestershire section of the line, but walkers and cyclists who carry on into Derbyshire, past the site of Melbourne station, will shortly come to a splendid bridge over the River Trent, a stone-built sarsen bridge over an old course of the river, and another bridge over the Trent & Mersey Canal. At Chellaston East Junction, just north of the bridges, the Ashby-Derby line joined another Midland line (Sheet Stores Junction to Stenson Junction) which provided an alternative route between Nottingham and Birmingham avoiding Derby. The Cloud Trail here leaves the trackbed, but continues into the very centre of Derby along the line of the former Derby Canal.

The Sheet Stores Junction to Stenson Junction line is still operational. These days it normally only carries freight but between 1869 and 1930 (the same dates as the Ashby-Derby line) it was a passenger service and the occasional passenger train is still sometimes re-routed this way to avoid engineering works. It had only one station in Leicestershire, at Castle Donington, which has been completely demolished.

3
Nuneaton to Ashby

By rail or canal

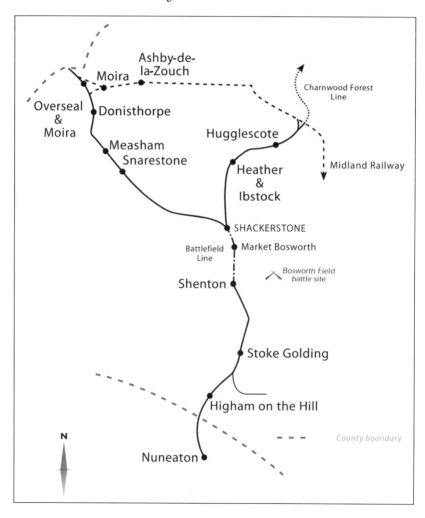

Ashby-de-la-Zouch

Moira

Overseal & Moira

Donisthorpe

Measham
Snarestone

Hugglescote

Charnwood Forest Line

Heather & Ibstock

Midland Railway

SHACKERSTONE

Battlefield Line

Market Bosworth

Bosworth Field battle site

Shenton

Stoke Golding

Higham on the Hill

N

County boundary

Nuneaton

Fierce rivalry between railway companies was the usual order of the day in Victorian England, but just occasionally they agreed to co-operate. The Ashby & Nuneaton Joint Railway was one such example, a collaboration between the London & North Western Railway (LNWR) and the Midland Railway.

The LNWR had already entered Leicester, in 1864, with a line from its stronghold of Nuneaton to Wigston, which is still open. Now the company wanted to thrust northwards from Nuneaton into the rich coalfields of the Charnwood Hills. The Midland Railway, alarmed, dusted off some old plans of its own and it looked as if competition would be fierce. In the end, however, the two companies decided on a joint venture.

Because of the intensity of farming in the southern part of the area traversed by the line, nearly a hundred bridges had to be constructed to carry the railway over country lanes and farm access tracks.

Although it was usually known as the Ashby & Nuneaton line, the town of Ashby was not, in fact, on the joint line as built. It was already on the Midland Railway's Leicester to Burton line (chapter 2) and was now linked to the new route by a triangular junction at Moira, over three miles away. Stations on the 29-mile line (Higham-on-the-Hill, Stoke Golding, Shenton, Market Bosworth, Shackerstone, Snarestone, Measham, Donisthorpe, and Overseal & Moira) were all built to a common pattern.

The opening ceremony took place on 16 August 1873, with a Feast and Sports Day at Market Bosworth for all those who had worked on the line. A special train ran from Nuneaton, with a band playing in the last wagon during the journey. The Royal Train, carrying Queen Victoria, travelled over the line in 1897 *en route* to Sheffield for the Diamond Jubilee celebrations.

Timetabled passenger services finished in 1931, the last train from Ashby to Shackerstone leaving on 11 April 1931. However, excursions continued to stop at local stations until the early 1960s. On 17 August 1969 the line was severed at its northern and southern ends (Moira West Junction and Weddington Junction), thereby effectively cutting it off from any through traffic. The track was removed between January and March 1972.

The route of the line, after leaving Nuneaton's Abbey Street station, entered Leicestershire a mile south-west of Higham-on-the-Hill station – traces can be seen from the A444 road (SK 360941) and from the A5 (SK 367950). Nuneaton is in Warwickshire, and while it still has a busy station on the West Coast main line, the old Abbey Street station no longer exists. However, its running-in board (the large sign as you enter a station) is preserved at the Shackerstone station museum and a totem (the smaller lozenge-shaped sign standardised by British Railways) is preserved at the Wheels Café at the surviving Nuneaton station.

The station building at Stoke Golding is now a riding school, and the stationmaster's house is a private residence. The goods sidings of the former station are mostly covered by the Willow Park Industrial Estate. However, there is a plaque erected by the roadside which recalls the railway.

Before Shenton the embankment to the south of the Ashby Canal is clearly visible, but public access is discouraged. From the canal to Shenton station, though, the trackbed has been turned into a footpath and nature reserve.

At Shenton, the situation becomes really positive. After closure of the line the rails were removed and Shenton

Market Bosworth station buildings, used by a car sales company. The railway is part of the restored Battlefield Line. (Judy Wheldon)

station demolished, but now the rails have been relaid. The station building from Leicester Humberstone Road (purchased for £1) was re-erected in 1993 brick by brick on the Shenton site by railway preservation enthusiasts and came back into service in 1996. It is a Grade II listed building. This is the southern end of the Battlefield Line, a restored heritage railway, which takes its name from the Battle of Bosworth Field. Shenton is only a short walk away from the site of the battle between the forces of Richard III and those of the Duke of Richmond (later Henry VII) in 1485, which ended the Wars of the Roses.

The next station was the biggest on the line. Market Bosworth was a market town, and a lot of agricultural produce passed through the station in the days before road transport became a major competitor. This meant it possessed ample sidings. The station buildings still stand, but are used as a car showroom. The stationmaster's house is a private residence. The Battlefield Line has acquired Platform 2 and the old LNWR signal box, but they are not open to the public, and the Line's trains simply pass through the station.

And so we come to Shackerstone (SK 379065). This was the key station, being the junction of the main Ashby & Nuneaton line with its branch line, which went through a

Shackerstone station's main building today. (Judy Wheldon)

more industrialised part of Leicestershire as far as Coalville Junction on the Midland Railway Leicester to Burton line. Shackerstone station was where the Ashby & Nuneaton Joint Railway had its headquarters.

It was also important from another point of view. Many distinguished guests, including King Edward VII and Queen Alexandra in 1902, used this station *en route* to and from Gopsall Hall, where they were guests of Lord Howe. In those days there was a handsome tree-lined approach to the station planted, it is said, by Lord Howe.

In its heyday Shackerstone was a busy junction station with, in 1922, a daily service of five passenger trains each

Florence no. 2, a 0-6-6 saddle tank, built by Bagnals of Stafford in 1953, stands at the head of a short train at Shackerstone station in 1978. (Leicester Mercury)

A general view of the restored Shackerstone station, taken from the footbridge linking the two platforms and showing much of the preservation society's rolling stock. (Judy Wheldon)

way running between Ashby and Nuneaton and one a day each way between Nuneaton and Burton. There were also motor trains between Shackerstone running up through its branch and on via the Charnwood Forest Line (see chapter 4) to Loughborough Derby Road.

Fortunately, the station buildings remained just about intact after closure long enough for them to be acquired by the Shackerstone Railway Society. In the summer of 1969 a small group of railway enthusiasts was trying to purchase an old Jubilee class locomotive. They failed in their endeavours, but did set up a society which went on to purchase a tank engine. They needed somewhere to keep it and were allowed to use part of the old line, near Market Bosworth. In early 1970 they moved to Shackerstone, where the station buildings had been neglected and vandalised. The society set about restoring the buildings to their old glory, while it purchased the trackbed between Shackerstone and Market Bosworth, and the station reopened in March 1978.

Then, in 1992, after much negotiation and energetic fund-raising, a further section running south to Shenton was acquired and in August that year came the proud moment when the first train for over 25 years steamed into Shenton station.

John C. Jacques, MBE, with some of the items from his collection. (Judy Wheldon)

A section of the old trackbed near Gopsall Wharf. (Judy Wheldon)

There is now a museum at Shackerstone station, containing an astonishing collection of some 3,000 items of railwayana (including 200 oil lamps). Many of them came from the doyen of the line, John C. Jacques MBE, a former signalman whose book *Railway Tales, Nostalgic Stories from the Age of Steam* relives some of the incidents from this railway.

Access to the station today is no longer, alas, by the handsome tree-lined route, but from a point north of the village of Shackerstone and the Ashby Canal and along the old trackbed. Brown tourist signs on nearby roads guide the car-borne visitor to the spot. The station is in typical Midland Railway style. The rebuilt waiting room on the down platform has been modelled on the original. The surviving iron footbridge probably dates from 1881.

Until 1923 the staff of the Ashby & Nuneaton Joint Railway had their own uniform, and the abbreviation ANJR was found on caps, buttons, etc. Under the 1923 Grouping the Nuneaton-Ashby line and its Shackerstone to Coalville branch came under the control of the London Midland & Scottish Railway (LMSR).

The main line continued towards the Moira junctions, where the trains joined the Midland Railway, using the West junction to Burton and the East junction to Ashby.

North of the Battlefield Line the trackbed is quite easy to follow and can be accessed from a car park at Gopsall Wharf. A pleasant circular walk (despite some brambles

Measham station, awaiting restoration. (Rodger Smith)

and nettles) is along the trackbed to the north, and back down the attractive Ashby Canal.

At Snarestone the station building has gone, though traces of the platform can be seen. The stationmaster's house is now a private residence, and the goods shed was recently converted to a dwelling.

South of Measham a local footpath leads off Ivanhoe Way into the station site. The station building is awaiting restoration to become a town museum (it was used for a time as a car repair garage). Unfortunately, the cast-iron verandah arches were cut away and stolen in around 1999. A terrace of railway workers' houses are now private residences. The goods shed has lost its loading canopy, but

The path has to start diverting from the line of the old trackbed here where the A42 slices across the route. (Rodger Smith)

apart from that has recently been sensitively converted for use by a boat-building firm.

The boat-building firm is here because there are plans to create an important marina on a reopened section of the Ashby Canal. The northern section of this canal, which had been affected by mining subsidence, was abandoned in 1944, but in 1966 an active restoration society was created. Around Measham parts of the old canal bed had been built over so the idea is, if sufficient funds can be raised, to re-route it along the line of the railway, rebuilding the old railway bridge as a canal aqueduct. It would be ironic if the canal were to use the old line, since it was the coming of the railway, running parallel over much the same route, which made the original canal uneconomic to maintain.

From the centre of Measham the track is easy to follow, since it now forms the Ashby Woulds Way cycleway and footpath, and, in part, the Ivanhoe Way, Mid-Leicestershire's long-distance footpath. At one point, however, the trackbed is sliced through by the modern A42 trunk road, and the path has to take a short diversion.

Donisthorpe station buildings have all gone. Some of the cuttings here were used for slurry lagoons of waste from Donisthorpe Colliery. Consequently, levels have changed. But the path follows more or less the line of the track, even if the gradient is different.

The track can be followed all the way to the Navigation Inn near the Moira West junction on the extant Leicester to Burton line. There is no trace of the Overseal & Moira station platforms or of the engine shed or the extensive sidings, but there is still a signal box there. Moira East junction runs by the edge of Conkers (National Forest Visitor Centre) in a tight curve on a high embankment.

Returning to Shackerstone, one can still see where the branch line to Coalville Junction went off in a north-easterly direction, but large parts of this route are in an area used for opencast mining.

Passenger services on the Shackerstone to Coalville branch began on 1 September 1873. The first station, Heather & Ibstock (now a coach garage), was also an important centre for freight, serving three brickworks.

The next station was Hugglescote, on the outskirts of Coalville, and although there is now no trace of the station, bits of the trackbed can still be discerned in the fields.

Although timetabled services on this Shackerstone to Coalville branch ceased in 1931, special excursions continued until the early 1960s. The line actually closed officially in 1964, though one enthusiasts' special ran through in 1965. The Ashby to Nuneaton line survived until the early 1970s.

The line now divides, one branch swinging to the north-west to join the tracks of the Leicester-Burton line to reach Coalville station while the other carries on northwards under a new name, the Charnwood Forest Railway, the subject of the next chapter.

4
The Bluebell Line

The Charnwood Forest Railway

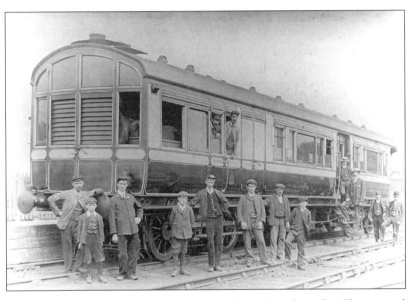

One of the independent steam coaches introduced to the Charnwood Forest Railway. This photograph is thought to have been taken at Loughborough Derby Road station, possibly at the time of their introduction. (Loughborough Library)

The prettiest line in Leicestershire, many people would say, was that of the Charnwood Forest Railway. This was often known as the Bluebell Line because of the profusion of bluebells growing in Grace Dieu Woods along the track.

No sooner had the Shackerstone to Coalville branch of the Joint Line (see chapter 3) been opened in 1873 than plans were laid to run a line between it and the important town of Loughborough.

The first sod of what was to become the Charnwood Forest Railway (CFR) was cut on 31 August 1881 by Lady Packe, of Prestwold Hall. Unfortunately, it was a day of rain. A local squire, Mr de Lisle, was supposed to wheel the first barrowload of soil away but he slipped off the plank provided and the barrow tipped over.

The railway, measuring 10¼ miles between Coalville Junction and Loughborough, was opened on 16 April 1883. Sections of the route followed approximately the course of the old Charnwood Forest Canal, crossing its now empty

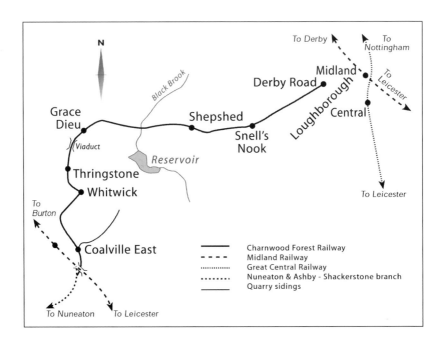

A photograph taken at Loughborough Derby Road station. (Loughborough Library)

channel bed several times. Because this line also went through some of the highest parts of Charnwood Forest, a number of cuttings had to be made through the sandstone hills.

The Charnwood Forest Railway was opened towards the end of the age of railway building. It was created and controlled by its own independent company, but with heavy investment from the LNWR, which ran the line. It continued in this fashion until the 1923 Grouping. It was never profitable, and from 1885 to 1909 it was actually in the hands of the Receiver. As one of a number of experiments aiming at more economic operation, a low-budget steam rail service was introduced in 1907 between Loughborough and Shackerstone, and three halts were opened, at Thringstone, Grace Dieu and Snells Nook, with platforms made up from old railway sleepers. Eventually, waiting huts were provided, but these halts were always very primitive.

One problem which prevented the company becoming economically viable was that it could never get the necessary authorisation to connect up with the Midland Railway main line in Loughborough, or with the Great Central Railway when that was built through Loughborough in 1898. Instead, the line had to end at its own isolated terminus, known as Loughborough Derby Road station. This meant that it never had the opportunity of carrying through traffic from the north.

The trackbed of the Charnwood Forest Line passing under the Leicester to Burton railway line. (Rodger Smith)

Regular passenger services ended in 1931, but holiday excursions continued until 1939. After that the CFR continued to get some income from freight traffic, particularly granite from the Whitwick Granite Company which had a direct rail connection to the southern end of the line. The last goods train ran from Shepshed to Coalville on 11 December 1963.

The line began at Coalville Junction and passed under a bridge carrying the Midland Railway's Leicester to Burton line. This bridge is still there, and the old trackbed can be accessed by a footpath southward which leaves the A511 road at SK 428134.

The approximate site of Coalville East station.

When the line was built, Coalville East station was outside the actual town. The station buildings were demolished in 1970 to make way for housing. New estates have now covered the whole area, but the route of the trackbed has largely been left as a grassed open space. A short alleyway, or 'jitty' in local parlance, leads from Charnwood Street and where this jitty emerges on to the grass is the site of the station, of which nothing now remains.

From that site, a new business park and a realignment of the A511 has obliterated the route of the old railway, until

The Whitwick station building, which is looked after by the Whitwick Historical Society, overlooks a footpath on the line of the old trackbed. (Rodger Smith)

it can be picked up again on the north-western side of a fishing lake, part of an attractive park. The line can then be followed as a footpath into Whitwick. The building, which was once the station, has been looked after by the Whitwick Historical Society since 1986.

Beneath Dumps Road bridge in Whitwick the trackbed is still there but densely overgrown. At the street called Whitwick Moor, now marked by a dense bed of nettles, was the site of Thringstone Halt, one of three request stops on the line. The halt consisted of a wooden platform and a small wooden building. No trace of the construction now remains, though for some years after the railway closed the building was used – according to local inhabitants – by a cobbler as a workshop.

The attractive viaduct in Grace Dieu woods. (Rodger Smith)

To the right of the trackbed is the Grace Dieu Trail, for pedestrians and cyclists, and this can be followed into the attractive Grace Dieu woods. The cuttings and the embankments of the track can be made out on the left. If you follow a path at the side of the trail (SK 431179), rather than the trail itself, you will emerge at one of the most impressive features of the lost railways of Leicestershire. This is the 120 ft long and 90 ft high Six Arches Viaduct in the middle of the wooded area.

Returning to follow the trackbed you cross the viaduct and continue on a high embankment until the ruins of Grace Dieu priory appear on the left. This walkable section of the route ends at the A512, the bridge over this road having long since disappeared. The trackbed continues on the other side but this is private land, firmly fenced off. However, immediately north of the road was the site of Grace Dieu halt.

The next chance to view the trackbed (here heavily overgrown) is from a bridge on Low Woods Lane, off the A512 about half a mile further to the east. The bridges over the track are all kept in good repair.

However, the best starting point for a viewing of some of the most dramatic trackbed scenery is from a lay-by on the A512 shortly before its junction with Tickow Lane (SK 458185). At the western end of this lay-by a footpath goes into the woods which quickly brings you to an impressive tunnel under a high embankment. This tunnel is not, as some reference books tell you, the old Charnwood Forest Canal, but was actually made under the canal for drovers to drive their cattle through. This is why it has a stone flagged floor, and the raised platforms at the side were not the towpath, but for the use of the drovers when the made roadway became flooded by the nearby Black Brook.

Climbing to the top of the old embankment brings you to the old railway line. A walk westwards will take you above the main course of the attractive Black Brook, formed by the overflow from the Blackbrook reservoir a few hundred yards to the south, though eventually the way is barred by a gate reinforced by tree trunks; beyond is private land.

However, walking in the other direction will bring you right into the south side of the small town of Shepshed. The path comes to an abrupt end at Charnwood Road, but on the opposite side a street has the name Old Station Close. The site of Shepshed station is now an industrial estate, but the keen eye may detect remains of the old platform edging.

The only reminder of the site of Shepshed station. (Rodger Smith)

Beyond this the line has been built over with modern housing, and though traces of it are to be found at the back of the truck stop these are inaccessible. Junction 23 of the M1 motorway cuts across the old line, but the route can be picked up again on the outskirts of Loughborough on the other side of the M1. The first point where it can be accessed is from Pitsford Drive, off Old Ashby Road, the latter being the first public road on the left of the A512. Westward from Pitsford Drive the track goes only a hundred yards or so before it is blocked by a mass of brambles and becomes impenetrable. In the easterly direction, however, the whole route has been preserved for a mile and a half as a cycle and pedestrian path, crossing street after street, including one, with picnic spot, which goes by the name of Trackside Close.

The end of the line was at Loughborough Derby Road station, the smallest of three stations which once stood in the town. The station itself was demolished in 1964, but the goods shed is still in use by a commercial company. The former existence of the station is, however, commemorated by two streets – Station Street and Station Avenue – and the imposing three-storey Station Hotel.

5
The Joint Line 1

Bottesford to Melton Mowbray

An inclined plane, part of the iron workings near Waltham-on-the-Wolds, which prompted the building of the route. (H.C. Casserley, Berkhamsted)

A grass bank is all that remains of Hose & Long Clawson station. This was on what was called the Joint Line, which ran north to south between Bottesford and Hallaton, with a westward branch into the city of Leicester itself. The grass bank is an excellent viewpoint. A large stretch of Leicestershire countryside lies before you. And there is hardly a house to be seen.

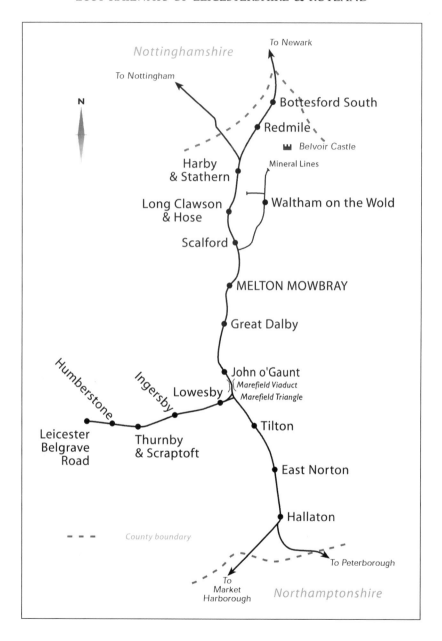

It is immediately apparent how rural this line was. No wonder, from a passenger traffic point of view, it was hopelessly uneconomic, even in the days before bus and car transport.

But then, as so often, minerals rather than passengers were the original motive for the coming of the railway. Ironstone deposits had been found at Waltham-on-the-Wolds and a local industrialist called William Frist, who had interests in the iron industry, decided a railway through the Leicestershire Wolds would be able to exploit the rich possibilities ironworking was offering in the mid 19th century.

Frist won supporters in the Yorkshire wool trade, whose own interest was in sending yarn to the Leicester hosiery

Eastwell Iron Ore Company locomotive pictured in 1960 near Waltham-on-the-Wolds. (H.C. Casserley, Berkhamsted)

factories, and who wanted an alternative to the Midland Railway route. They came together to form the Newark & Leicester Railway Company, and produced plans for a line.

However, this was the second great period of railway expansion, and both the Great Northern Railway and the Midland Railway were also casting covetous eyes on the Leicestershire iron ore resources.

Great Northern got to the fledgling Newark & Leicester Railway first, and took it over in 1871. There were problems getting permission through Parliament to build the line, because at first members of the House of Lords rejected the southern part of the route (Melton to Leicester), thinking it would interfere with their hunting. Leicestershire has always been renowned as England's premier county for fox hunting.

In 1872 the Great Northern built the line from Bottesford Junction (where it joined its own Nottingham to Grantham route) to Melton Mowbray, and also created at the northern end a western spur (owned jointly with the LNWR) from Saxondale Junction (also on the Nottingham to Grantham line) to Stathern Junction. A few years later it also added its Bottesford to Newark line.

For the purposes of this county-based book the line could not have started at a more convenient location, since Bottesford is the most northerly settlement in Leicestershire. Bottesford South station, however, only remained open for three years, because passengers were very few.

Going south, the line gave a dramatic view of Belvoir Castle (home of the Duke of Rutland) which, situated on its high ridge, dominates the skyline. The Duke, who was a hunting enthusiast, had at first been one of the foremost opponents of the proposal for the line, but later withdrew his opposition, having realised that ironstone working on parts of his vast lands would greatly benefit his purse.

The Duke's predecessor had been a railway pioneer. An early horse-drawn railway had run into a tunnel under the castle itself. This line, with 4 ft 4½ inch gauge, had been built by the Butterley Iron Company in 1815 to bring coal to the castle from the Grantham Canal, two miles away. There are still sections of the original fish-bellied rails visible in the castle grounds, and these are thought to be the oldest cast iron railway lines anywhere in the country still in their original position. Another piece of the track is at the National Railway Museum in York.

The nearest point on the line to Belvoir Castle was to the west of the small village of Redmile. Redmile station, though serving a sparse rural community, was therefore given a magnificent station fit for a duke and his visitors. There was a *porte-cochère* at the front of the building to shelter the notables when they got into their carriages or alighted from them, and an ornate seven-gable platform canopy. The duke had a private waiting room, equipped with a grand oak fireplace and carved scene of a hunt in full cry. But, despite all this grandeur, the station closed in 1951 and was demolished.

Next down the line was Harby & Stathern station (opened 1879), situated midway between the two villages, three quarters of a mile south of Stathern Junction. It had an extra platform because of the junction, with trains going east to Grantham or west to Nottingham. The station, which also had extensive sidings to take iron ore wagons, closed on 7 December 1953, and the land is now used for industrial purposes.

Southwards from Stathern the line climbed up to the hills of the Leicestershire Wolds, then through a tunnel and

The site of Waltham station today. (Rodger Smith)

a deep cutting to reach a valley which led to Melton Mowbray. On this stretch there were stations at Hose & Long Clawson (opened and closed the same days as Harby & Stathern) and Scalford.

The Hose & Long Clawson station was more inconvenient than usual, being situated two miles from each village. It had been built in similar style to the station at Harby & Stathern.

Scalford station was at least closer to its community. South of the station a branch ran off to the north-east to access Waltham-on-the-Wold and nearby iron ore workings. A station was opened in 1883 at Waltham-on-the-Wold but was only used for occasional passenger services (such as hunt meets), and never appeared in regular timetables.

In the 1880s a man named Jimmy Carrington, who was travelling on the 1.53 pm train out of Nottingham to Northampton, put his head out of the carriage and was struck by a bridge. He was killed instantly, and for many years afterwards the 1.53 pm train was known as the 'Jimmy Carrington'.

This particular train seems to have been jinxed, because on 25 July 1892, 200 yards north of Melton Mowbray North station, there was an accident when the same 1.53 pm derailed and rolled down a 22-ft embankment. The driver and his fireman, and a boy passenger, were killed.

Melton Mowbray was the main town on the line, and the Great Northern made sure that their station, Melton Mowbray North, was an imposing showpiece, in red brick with lavish ornamentation and gables, cast iron stanchions and glass canopies. It also had a wide subway in vitrified white brick. Until 1912 this station housed the office of the Joint Superintendent of the line. There was a range of waiting rooms and refreshment rooms. The GNR badge from here is now preserved at Leicester Museum of Technology. As in other stations, the glass was removed from the canopies during the Second World War for safety reasons, and was not replaced until several years after the war ended in 1945.

In addition to passenger and general freight, the line also carried a lot of cattle (including special cattle trains) to and from Melton Mowbray; fortunately the cattle market was situated near the station. Melton Mowbray was, of course, one of the great hunting centres, and fox-hunters would keep their horses in hunting lodges in the town or close to it and would have them sent to the station on the line

Melton Mowbray station, with glass missing from the canopies.
(H.C. Casserley, Berkhamsted)

nearest the meet. These huntsmen and women came from as far afield as London (or even further: one of the most enthusiastic was the Maharajah of Cooch Behar).

What of the line today? South of Bottesford much of the trackbed is still there, though largely inaccessible. Where it can be reached it is densely overgrown, mostly with brambles and hawthorn, which makes it practically impenetrable. But because the route of the line is still almost intact, if it could only be cleared it would make a splendid long-distance cycle path. The best way to explore this section of the line is probably by bicycle, because there are not many convenient places to park a car.

A visitor to a point at the west end of Bottesford village (SK 798392) will see a lane running northwards, and some 200 yards along it, arms sweep off on either side to go to

The entrance to the refreshment room at Melton Mowbray station, 1953, showing both LMS and LNER poster boards. (H.C. Casserley, Berkhamsted)

the junctions with the Nottingham to Grantham line. The lane is on trackbed, and the railway authorities, as a sign indicates, seem to believe that the railway is still there.

Going southwards, the trackbed passes under the A52 road but the next point at which it is possible to get a good view of it is from a bridge close to the site of Redmile station, west of Redmile village (SK 787362). An even closer view can be obtained at Barkestone-le-Vale village, where a narrow lane past the church leads down to two adjoining bridges, one over the Grantham Canal and the other over the old railway.

Here the devoted railway rambler (and the numbers of these are growing every year) will look with envy on the smooth grassway alongside the Grantham Canal, kept

Wishful thinking. This sign, near Bottesford, is at the entrance to a narrow lane which was the trackbed of the old railway. But the rails have long since disappeared.

mown for the benefit of horse-riders, a contrast to the dense undergrowth encumbering the railway track.

A narrow road between Plungar and Harby has two bridges, the first over the line from Bottesford and the second over the connecting line from Saxendale Junction (this line, mainly in Nottinghamshire, was covered in an earlier book in this series, *Lost Railways of Nottinghamshire*). From these bridges you can clearly see the 'V' junction where the two lines join (SK 762324), but there is no way anyone other than a party armed with machetes, determination and time could make their way to the junction point through the dense growth on either line.

At the T-junction with the Harby to Stathern road you can turn left under a bridge which took the railway over the road. On the other side is a track leading south to Station Farm, and the site of Harby & Stathern station. The track and the site are private property, and protected by iron gates and railings.

A road (Hose Lane) leads between the villages of Hose and Long Clawson. If you take a narrow road (with a sign stating 'Unsuitable for heavy vehicles') called Pasture Lane, this will eventually bring you to a group of houses (SK 745271), some of which were built by the railway company. At the back of the building known as Station Farm there is a footpath (with a waymark sign) going across two fields. The line of this path is by no means clear on the ground, but a more or less straight course leads to a waymarked stile in a hedge. The large area of level open ground on the other side of the stile is the site of Hose & Long Clawson station, and the line of the trackbed can be clearly made out towards the north.

This open area is surrounded by the rising ground known generally as the Harby Hills and here, in particular, as Brock Hill. The only major tunnel on the line goes through Brock Hill. This 834-yard long tunnel, which is still in excellent condition – though unfortunately not on any footpath – emerges to the south in a deep wide cutting. This cutting can be viewed (SK 747254) from Landyke Lane, an even narrower gated road between Scalford and Long Clawson. But be warned! You will see a sight that will make the heart of the railway enthusiast sink. For this has now become a landfill site, and presumably one day the cutting will be no more and perhaps even the tunnel, a superb piece of Victorian engineering, lost for ever.

The southern entrance to the tunnel through Brock Hill. (Rodger Smith)

Moving now to Scalford, the approach road to what was the site of the station still joins the Scalford to Melton road (SK 757241), but is now occupied by modern industrial buildings belonging to a waste reclamation company.

After Scalford the trackbed runs all the way to Melton Mowbray near the bottom of a steep valley created by the Scalford Brook. The trackbed is actually a feature of the Melton Country Park, on the north-east edge of Melton Mowbray (car parking and visitor centre at SK 758208), and at last access to it is easy and walkable.

However, south of the park, where the line used to make a wide curve to the south-west, the prospect is depressing. The line's showpiece station, Melton Mowbray North, has completely disappeared. After closure, this once great building was declared a local eyesore. In April 1966 Melton Urban District Council agreed to buy the 67-acre disused property and the station, together with the adjoining bridge over Scalford Road, was demolished in 1970 and the site cleared. A car park for a Co-operative supermarket and some industrial buildings now occupy the site.

6
The Joint Line 2

Melton Mowbray to Hallaton and Leicester

The 1.55 pm to Leicester, leaving John o' Gaunt station in January 1942. (H.C. Casserley, Berkhamsted)

After Melton Mowbray, going south, the line described in the last chapter curved round and passed over the Midland Railway's Syston to Peterborough and Nottingham to Melton lines and entered the rolling country known as the Wolds. This meant greater engineering problems, with cuttings and embankments, to keep to a certain gradient.

In Melton Mowbray itself the line of the trackbed can be picked up again today from the west side of Nottingham

The Marefield 13-arch viaduct, south of John o' Gaunt station. (Rodger Smith)

Road, where a stretch of embankment is intact and is used as a path. The bridge which took the track over Asfordby Road has now gone, but the embankment can be found again on the other side of this road, and followed as far as the River Wreake. The old railway bridge over the river has been demolished, but the abutments can still be seen. There is now a modern footbridge on the same alignment, but south of the river the trackbed enters farmland, not all of it accessible, though still in parts traceable on a map.

You can pick up its traces again on the other side of Kirkby Lane, running southwards towards Dalby. The bridge that took the railway over the minor road between

The down platform at Lowesby station, pictured in August 1953.
(H.C. Casserley, Berkhamsted)

Great Dalby and Ashby Folville is still there. This is called
Station Road, and on the right are Station Cottages. The
site of Great Dalby station is now used by an egg-
producing firm.

The railway, after passing through a deep cutting at
Thorpe Trussels, came to a station which opened on
15 December 1879 as Burrow & Twyford, though situated
at some distance from the two villages (Burrow is now
known as Burrough on the Hill). In 1883 the station was
renamed John o' Gaunt, after a famous fox covert situated
about a mile to the south. It is thought to be the only station
in the country named for its fox-hunting connections!

John o' Gaunt station was just before Marefield junction,
where one line branched westwards to run into Leicester

The former Lowesby station buildings undergoing extensive rebuilding as a private residence, but incorporating many original features. (Rodger Smith)

Belgrave Road station, and the other continued due south to Hallaton. It closed to normal passenger traffic on 7 December 1953, but an unadvertised workmen's train continued to run from the station until April 1957. John o' Gaunt station buildings have now been converted to industrial premises.

By retracing your steps and taking a minor road off Station Hill (SK 736097) you soon find coming into view one of the most striking features of this section of the line, the 13-arch Marefield Viaduct. The viaduct carries the route across a broad valley created by a now modest

The stationmaster's house, Ingarsby. (Rodger Smith)

stream. A bridle path (SK 739091) will take you right to the viaduct itself for a closer look. There are splendid views from the top.

The trackbed is easily traceable south to the Marefield junction, which forms an almost perfect triangle. This was where the GNR line to the city of Leicester branched off.

Let us start by taking this line running west to Leicester. The first station reached is Lowesby, south of the village, opened in 1882 and closed in December 1953 (though the workmen's special from John o' Gaunt called until April 1957). The buildings and platforms have survived and are being sensitively restored as a private residence.

The remains of an old signal box at Ingarsby. (Rodger Smith)

The next station was Ingarsby, the name of a lost village, though the site of it was close to the railway line. The name was a curious choice, the place being so insignificant, but the station was midway between two surviving villages, Hungarton and Houghton on the Hill. Still to be seen at Ingarsby are a large bridge abutment and part of an embankment, the top of which is accessible. On the other side of the road, down a side road, is the old stationmaster's house. It is now a private residence, but has a plaque recording its former use. There are also plans to restore the signal box nearby.

The route continued towards Leicester, and had a tunnel and a stone viaduct between Ingarsby and Thurnby, so it

Still looking very rural, Thurnby & Scraptoft station in August 1953. Note that the design of the station is almost identical to that of Lowesby. (H.C. Casserley, Berkhamsted)

could negotiate undulating ground conditions. Thurnby tunnel became notorious for the giant icicles which formed round the ventilation shafts in cold winter weather, and the first train of the day had to smash through these. The course of the line, which so far has been easy enough to trace on modern Ordnance Survey maps, disappears from view as we near the outer suburbs of Leicester.

Thurnby & Scraptoft was the station for two villages which are now both suburbs of the city, but were rural when the line was built. It was much nearer Thurnby but Scraptoft was the bigger village. The station has gone, though there is a Station Road in Thurnby, and the stationmaster's house, now a private residence, is still there.

By the early 1900s the suburbs of Leicester had already spread out to the next station, Humberstone. These days Humberstone is so much a part of the city that it is hardly thought of as a separate district, but then it was still a self-sufficient community. The station has completely disappeared, but the stationmaster's house is still in use as a private residence.

In the 1980s a remaining open area in the Humberstone area (car parking off Abbotsford Road) became a park, recreation ground and nature reserve. The nature reserve, now managed by the environmental charity Environ, includes a section of the railway embankment (accessed by

Humberstone station, with its wooden platforms, pictured in 1953. (H.C. Casserley, Berkhamsted)

Humberstone stationmaster's house, now a private residence. (Rodger Smith)

steps from the park), which has been given the name of Rally Bank.

And then the branch finally ran into its terminus, at Leicester Belgrave Road. This station was built as a prestige project, because it marked the entry by the Great Northern Railway into a city which had previously been a Midland Railway preserve. It was only three-quarters of a mile from the city centre. There were two train sheds, five platforms, a spacious concourse with three large entrances, and a grand clock tower with an onion-shaped cupola. The frontage was created in what was called the Jacobean Revival style. A feature was a parapet with nine ornate gables. The brickwork was orange in colour, with

Rally Bank, a piece of trackbed in a corner of the Humberstone Park recreation ground which has been preserved as a nature reserve. (Rodger Smith)

terracotta ornamentation. A subway connected the different platforms.

The first train, which pulled out of the station on 2 October 1882, was an excursion to Skegness. The Lincolnshire holiday resorts of Skegness and Mablethorpe were always favourites for Leicester people, and Belgrave Road station became known as the 'station for the sea'. In 1959 over 20,000 people travelled to the two resorts in 72 trains; in sad symmetry, the last train to travel the line, in September 1962, was also a Skegness special. There were daily services for Grantham, Newark and Peterborough. Trains to Peterborough ended in 1916.

Leicester's Belgrave Road station when it was fully operational. (H.C. Casserley, Berkhamsted)

An early photograph of Leicester Belgrave Road station. (Leicestershire Museums, Arts and Records Service)

After closure the site of the Belgrave Road station became a fairground, then a car breaker's yard, and the station buildings were finally demolished in the early 1970s. A Sainsbury's supermarket was built on the site. There is now nothing to be seen, because of major road developments in the area. One of the slip roads for the Belgrave Road flyover actually stands on the site of the old booking hall.

The only Leicester station that still exists as part of the main line network is Leicester London Road station, built by the Midland Railway in 1895 to replace an earlier 1840 building. As it is fully used today for both long-distance and local traffic, and most of its features are intact, it lies outside the province of this book but it, too, nearly became a lost station. When the station buildings were threatened with demolition in the 1970s they were only saved by local protests.

Let us now return to the Marefield triangle, and the route running south. The course of the line, still obvious, crosses farmland, but at a point (SK 762056) on the Tilton to Oakham road is Tilton Cutting. The railway here was hewn through rock, and the strata which have been exposed are of great interest to those with a geological bent. The particular nature of the cutting attracts birds and butterflies, and it has been designated a Site of Special Scientific Interest. Steps lead down into the cutting, and interpretation boards have been provided.

The station here took its name from Tilton-on-the-Hill village two miles away, ignoring the hamlet of Halstead, even though Tiltonians had to pass through Halstead to reach their station. A private house now occupies the site.

For some way between Tilton and Loddington the line runs parallel with the road. At Oxley crossroads there is a substantial bridge where you can look down to a deep cutting. Some parts of the trackbed are walkable, others have been used for farm purposes (a manure heap blocks the track at one point).

The railway was now squeezing its way between hills, with the delightfully named Whatborough Hill and Robin-a-Tiptoe to the east and Round Hill to the west. A bridlepath from the Hallaton to East Norton road will take you along a ridge and the line of the trackbed can be seen below. It passes through the ridge by a tunnel, with no public access.

The village of Loddington, though its church and hall were adjacent to the railway, was never deemed important enough to merit a station. Residents would have to make their way two miles to the south, to East Norton station (adjacent, then as now, to the A47 road). No trace of the station remains.

On the Loddington to East Norton road there is access to the trackbed at a point where substantial bridge abutments can be seen. There is quite a walkable length here, running westwards. East Norton also had a viaduct comparable to that of Marefield, but it was judged dangerous and was blown up on 25 March 2001. There is nothing much left in East Norton itself, apart from the colour of the bricks on the A47 road, which shows where a bridge once stood.

Just east of the village of Hallaton on the very narrow Allexton road you can see the abutments of the railway bridge and it is possible to go up to the top of the embankment. Here a metal gate bars access to horses or vehicles, and a sign makes it clear that it is private land, but those wishing to walk the track may do so at their own risk except one day a year, on 1 November. The

Leicester Belgrave Road station in wartime. The 1 pm train to John o'
Gaunt is about to depart on 10 January 1942.

countryside here is very undulating, but the railway keeps
its gradients, usually by embankments.

Passing very quickly from a high embankment with
extensive views to being on a level with the neighbouring
fields, or even going into a cutting, gives you an
appreciation of the difficulties experienced by the railway
builders when they had to keep their level gradient.
Several handsome bridges go over the track on this route,
all for farm access and all in apparently good repair.
However, as this permissive path nears the ridge through
which the tunnel went, it is firmly fenced off.

Hallaton village is famous for its Easter bottle-kicking
ritual, one of those strange old customs which have
survived since time immemorial. Special trains brought
spectators to this event in the past. The station, which for

The south portal of an extant railway tunnel between East Norton and Hallaton. (Rodger Smith)

A course for training horses to jump fences, a novel use for an old railway cutting between Hallaton and East Norton. (Rodger Smith)

once was conveniently near the village, has been demolished and a modern bungalow, known as The Old Station, stands on the site.

With the gradient now dropping as the line moves towards the broad valley of the River Welland, Hallaton was the final station on the joint line before it split, one section going east towards Peterborough, the other south-west towards Market Harborough.

LNWR ran trains between Nottingham and Northampton, calling at Melton Mowbray and Market Harborough, six each way daily. Its engines were usually kept in the sheds at the big LNWR depot at Colwick in Nottinghamshire.

97

The GNR passenger service from Leicester Belgrave Road to Grantham, Newark and Peterborough suffered from passing through mainly rural areas. In the 20th century buses provided serious competition, because of the long walks from villages to stations. Passenger trains were withdrawn in 1953, the last train from Market Harborough to Melton Mowbray running on 5 December 1953 to some ceremony.

Despite its commercial failure as a passenger line, the joint line was very successful as a freight route. Ironstone formed the bulk of its traffic, supplemented by coal and farm produce. All goods traffic between Nottingham and Melton ceased in September 1964, although some parts of the joint line survived longer.

7
Lines into and out of Rutland

Rutland may be Britain's smallest county, but it has never lost its fiercely independent spirit. It has now recovered, as a unitary authority, the administrative autonomy it once enjoyed as a county council.

The only station open in Rutland today is at Oakham, the county town. But in the heyday of railways it was the small village of Manton, rather than Oakham itself, which served as Rutland's most important junction.

The Midland Railway's Syston Junction to Peterborough line was completed in 1846, a west-to-east route which followed a winding route designed to take in the three market towns of Melton Mowbray (Leicestershire), Oakham (Rutland) and Stamford (Lincolnshire). Passenger trains still run on this line, and stop at Melton Mowbray and Stamford, but in Rutland itself Oakham is the only stop. All intermediate stations, as well as Syston itself, had been closed by 1961.

Syston railway station buildings, however, are being returned to railway use, though on a different site. The original structure was erected in 1875 to a classic three-pavilion design, including a booking office, booking hall, waiting rooms and toilets. After closure the premises were used for various purposes, but eventually the whole site was bought by a single purchaser for redevelopment. He offered the station building to the Midland Railway Trust, which runs a heritage railway on a former industrial line at Butterley in Derbyshire (www.midland railwaycentre.co.uk). The Syston

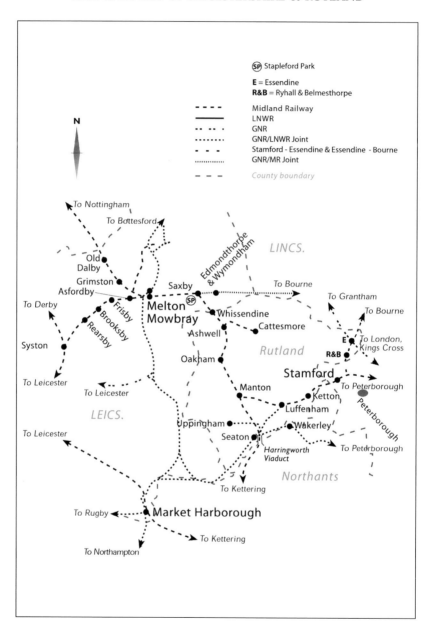

station building was dismantled brick by brick, to be re-erected at the Swanwick Junction end of the Trust's railway.

The Rearsby station platforms have gone but the station buildings have survived more or less intact and now form part of a private residence. The buildings at Brooksby station are also intact (and Grade II listed), and are looked after by Leicestershire County Council. At Frisby the buildings have been removed, as they have at Asfordby station (which was similar in design to Rearsby).

Trains still run into Melton Mowbray Town, one of two stations to serve Melton, but the only one now to survive (the other was on the GNR-LNWR line from Bottesford to Melton, see chapter 5). When that station was opened in 1879, the Midland Railway set about making their own more imposing, and its most attractive feature, the three-arched Italianate frontage, was added soon after 1879. Platform glass canopies were also installed at the same time.

After Melton came Saxby, a village close to Stapleford Park, home in the 1840s of the irascible Earl of Harborough, an implacable opponent of the new-fangled railway idea. This was where the 'Battle of Saxby', actually a series of minor skirmishes, took place in 1844.

The Midland Railway wanted to lay down a course for the Syston to Peterborough line which took advantage in its Leicestershire section of the valleys of the rivers Eye and Wreake. The River Eye flows down from the low hills south-east of Melton Mowbray and through the middle of Stapleford Park before turning due west to enter Melton Mowbray. There it flows into the River Wreake, which continues gently in a south-westerly direction to Syston and on to enter the River Soar.

The railway made an approach to Lord Harborough to see if he would sell any of his land. His response was a definite no, but he did not stop there. He immediately put up notices all round his estate stating that any attempt by the railway surveyors to enter Stapleford Park would be met by force.

On 13 November 1844, seven Midland Railway surveyors with their support staff were walking towards Stapleford Park along the towpath of the Oakham Canal. This canal, between Oakham and Melton Mowbray, had been built in 1802, and Lord Harborough was a major shareholder. It was destined to be doomed by the competition from the railway and, in fact, was abandoned almost as soon as the railway opened, in 1846.

Lord Harborough's men stopped the Midland Railway team and ordered them to go back. The surveyors refused, as the towpath was open to public access. However, the Harborough men, who were armed, arrested the survey team and put them into a cart with the intention, it seems, of bringing them before a magistrate. A policeman stopped them and pointed out that what they were doing was unlawful. So the Harborough men tipped the railwaymen onto the road.

Next day the Midland Railway men returned in force, some 40 in number, with the surveyors this time supported by powerfully-built navvies from Stamford and even prize-fighters from Nottingham. But the Harborough team had also been reinforced, and a general fracas resulted, with men on both sides tumbling into a filthy ditch. The railway contingent were then chased away back down the towpath.

Two days later the Midland Railway men were back, this time in the early morning, but again the Harborough men were waiting, and there was another free-for-all. The railway people came off worse, with injuries and with their equipment smashed. The authorities had to take note and some navvies were sent to prison for riotous behaviour, while some of Lord Harborough's men were fined for damaging the surveying equipment.

On 30 June 1845 the Midland Railway got its Act through Parliament to build the line, but Lord Harborough still did all he could to hamper construction. On 28 November there was another brawl, with his Lordship this time involved, driving a carriage at full speed into the opposition of 150 railwaymen.

The severe curve that had to be created to avoid Lord Harborough's land was a major problem, slowing trains, but by 1880 Lord Harborough was dead and Stapleford Park had another owner. This owner was more reasonable, and allowed the Midland Railway to build an easier curve.

Once this problem was solved the Midland Railway created, in 1893, a new line to Bourne in Lincolnshire, and Saxby thereby became a junction. It was part of a new joint system operated by the Midland and Great Northern. The Leicestershire section of this railway can still be traced on the map, but is difficult to access. A Leicestershire station existed at Edmondthorpe & Wymondham (the station buildings have been converted to a bungalow).

Passenger services began in 1894 with three local trains a day each way, but these were uneconomic from the start, because the Lincolnshire section of the line was very thinly populated. Long-distance trains from Leicester and Nottingham, especially summer excursions to the East Anglian resorts of Great Yarmouth, Cromer and Hunstanton, were more successful. In 1959 passenger facilities were withdrawn, and eventually the rails were lifted between Saxby Junction and Bourne, except for a quarry section near Market Overton.

The Midland Railway's 'Melton line', a major north-south route to London, which ran from Nottingham to Melton Mowbray and then down to Kettering, used a section of the west to east Syston to Peterborough line through Oakham and then as far as Manton Junction. There it separated from the Syston-Peterborough line to run south to Kettering, where it joined the Midland main line coming down from Derby via Trent Junction.

Between Nottingham and Melton Mowbray there were two stations in the Leicestershire section: Old Dalby, which opened on 2 February 1880 and remained open till 18 April 1966, and Grimston, also opened in February 1880 but which closed on 4 February 1957. The station at Grimston was actually nearer the village of Saxelby, but the name was not used because of its similarity to Saxby.

The Melton line was severed at its northern (Nottingham) end as a result of the Beeching closures, but became a twelve-mile rail test track from a point in southern Nottinghamshire as far as the Asfordby Junction, west of Melton Mowbray. This track was used for testing the Advanced Passenger Train and the Pendolinos.

South of Melton Mowbray, along the line, and now into Rutland, Whissendine station has closed and disappeared, though the road out of Whissendine which led to it is known as Station Road and there are still Station Cottages near the site, marked today by a level crossing and signal box. Ashwell station has also disappeared. It was where a former mineral branch line came in to join the main line.

Today that branch line does not connect up with the main line, but part of it still exists to form the core of the Rutland Railway Museum (SK 886137), near Cottesmore, which occupies an area of nearly seven acres. It concentrates on industrial locomotives and rolling stock, especially that from local ironstone quarry railways. There is a visitor centre and shop, and it is open summer weekends and some other times (www.rutnet.co.uk).

After Oakham the line moves south to Manton Junction, with Manton station sited just before the junction. Manton also acted as the Midland Railway's station for Uppingham (3½ miles away), with its well-known public school. The station was actually listed as 'Manton for Uppingham' until 1934. Timetabled passenger trains were withdrawn from this line in June 1960, though specials to Uppingham School, and freight services, continued until May 1964.

At Manton Junction the old Midland line to Kettering ran due south, while the Syston-Peterborough line branched off to the east. The creation of the junction when the Nottingham to Kettering line opened in 1880 turned the station into an important interchange. Platforms were inserted inside the 'V' of the junction, alongside the now diverging lines, with a metal footbridge on brick piers connecting them all up.

Both are still there today, but only the Syston-Peterborough line carries passenger traffic. Manton station has gone, though some of the buildings are used for industrial purposes.

The former main line south of Manton, the Kettering line, remains open for freight, and contains the Harringworth viaduct over the broad valley of the River Welland: at 3,825 ft long, 57 ft high, with 82 arches (each with a 40 ft span), it is the longest rural viaduct in Britain, and the biggest masonry rail structure in Europe. It was built between 1874 and 1879, and 2,500 men were employed during the construction. Brickworks, using local clay, had to be set up at either end, and eventually more

The Harringworth viaduct striding across the landscape. The building in the foreground is the former Seaton station. (Rodger Smith)

than 20 million bricks were used. The viaduct could be seen clearly from Seaton station, and is today one of the most impressive railway structures in the country. It is also known as the Seaton Viaduct or the Welland Viaduct.

The best place to get an overall view is from a lay-by on the Harringworth to Caldecott road (SP 907954). This viewpoint is evidently so popular that picnic tables have now been installed on the adjoining strip of grass.

A 19th century clergyman, the Rev. D.W. Barratt, wrote a book about the workmen who built the Harringworth viaduct, *Life and Work among the Navvies*. A facsimile reprint is available from the Gretton Local History Society

Seaton station, looking west. (H.C. Casserley, Berkhamsted)

(www.kellner.eclipse.co.uk). A huge repair project on the viaduct, which will take three years and cost £1.5 million, started in 2005.

The LNWR ran a line from Market Harborough to Peterborough passing through Seaton, and a branch was run from there into the centre of Uppingham town. Much of the trackbed for this line is still there, and in many places can be seen clearly from the B672 Caldecott to Morcott road.

Seaton station is now a private residence, though it retains the station canopies, the down waiting room, the platforms and even the old iron footbridge. Next door, the old station yard is now being used for scrap metal handling. Uppingham station, at the end of the branch, is the site of an industrial estate.

About a mile and a half north of Seaton is the Morcott tunnel, still intact and in an excellent state of repair. Access,

The Seaton station footbridge and station building today, on private land. (Rodger Smith)

however, is difficult, requiring a perilous descent down a steep embankment just off a lay-by on the main A47 road (926004) and a push through undergrowth at the bottom.

The LNWR Market Harborough to Peterborough line, which connected with the Midland Railway's line at North Luffenham, ended in 1966. The last part of the trackbed, between South and North Luffenham, has been designated as a permissive footpath. Encouragingly, part of the eastern end of this line at Peterborough is operated by the Nene Valley heritage railway, but this is beyond the Rutland county boundary and so falls outside the scope of this book.

The north portal of Morcott tunnel. (Rodger Smith)

Luffenham station when it was still in operation. (H.C. Casserley, Berkhamsted)

The old trackbed of the LNWR Market Harborough to Peterborough line approaching its junction with the surviving Midland line at North Luffenham. (Rodger Smith)

At the eastern extremity of Rutland is the village of Essendine, which lies on the Great Northern Railway's main line (known today as the East Coast main line). Its GNR station remained open from 1852 to 1959. The nearby town of Stamford in Lincolnshire, which from its proximity to the Great North Road (today the A1) had been a major coaching centre, had turned its back on railways when they first came upon the scene, and been bypassed. Determined to make up for missing out on the early development, its major landowner, the Marquess of Exeter (who owned Burghley House), promoted his own line

*Part of the Ryhall & Belmesthorpe station platform can still be seen.
(Rodger Smith)*

from a junction with the GNR line at Essendine and into
Stamford. This 12½ mile double track route opened on
1 November 1856, with an intermediate station at Ryhall &
Belmesthorpe (also in Rutland). This gave Stamford a
connection to Kings Cross until the line closed in 1929.

There is also a 6½-mile lost line (opened 1860, closed
1959), traceable on a map, between Essendine and Bourne,
but all except the first mile of this is in Lincolnshire.

8

Lost lines to Rugby and Northampton

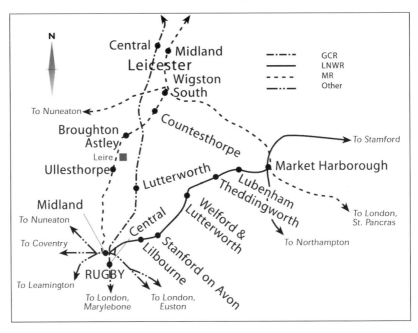

In the days before the railway age, the town of Market Harborough was an important stopping and changing post for stage coaches, situated as it is at the junction of the north-south Carlisle to London road and the east-west Rugby to Stamford road. And when the railways came, for a century and more, it was an important rail junction serving more or less the same routes.

Welford & Lutterworth station at North Kilworth seen before closure.
(H.C. Casserley, Berkhamsted)

One of the lines, the old Midland Railway line between London St Pancras and the North, is still as busy as ever, and the platforms at Market Harborough station are well patronised by commuters and shoppers on their way to and from the metropolis. For Market Harborough is noted as one of the more desirable places in England to live, and a direct line to London is part of the attraction.

But until recently there were other platforms at this same station, serving lines to Rugby, Stamford and Northampton. They became disused when these routes were lost in 1966, and the space they occupied was eventually used for an extension to the station car park.

These disused platforms belonged to the LNWR, which had been the first railway company into Market

113

Harborough. They built the first station in 1849, and when the Midland Railway started to use it they had to pay fees to the LNWR. As traffic increased the two companies agreed to build a joint station. This opened on 14 September 1884. From a passing train you can only see it at an angle, because the railway here runs on a high embankment, but from street level you will find a most unusual building, in what is called a Queen Anne style. It survives in all its glory, and is now recognised as one of the architectural ornaments of Market Harborough.

But our task is to trace the lost lines, not today's busy mainline, and we therefore need to go back to that first LNWR connection to Market Harborough.

The old LNWR line comes north to Market Harborough from Rugby by following the valley of the River Avon, which in this area forms the boundary between Leicestershire and Warwickshire. The line crossed the river (and into Leicestershire) south of the village of North Kilworth, and a station was created a mile east of the village, where the railway crossed the Lutterworth to Market Harborough road. This, now the A4304, is called Station Road at this point – and nearby there is also a Station Farm. It is thought that the LNWR had wanted to build a station two miles further along, next to the more important village of Husbands Bosworth, but the owners of Highcroft House, a large estate, objected to having a railway station so close to them.

Husbands Bosworth's loss was therefore North Kilworth's gain, but not in name. The LNWR decided that North Kilworth was too insignificant and so, astonishingly, they gave the station the name of Welford & Lutterworth. Astonishingly, because Welford was a Northamptonshire village four miles away to the south-east as the crow flies, but even further away by road, for there was no direct route linking the village and the station. As for the Leicestershire town of Lutterworth, this was an important centre in Victorian times, but it was nine miles away to the west.

The site of the station is now used for industrial purposes, and there is no direct access to the trackbed at North Kilworth. But an attractive parallel walk will also pass a remarkable engineering feat from the canal age. By following the towpath of the Grand Union Canal northwards from North Kilworth you arrive at the mouth

The Brampton Valley Way cycle path follows the route of the old LNWR line from Market Harborough to Northampton. (Judy Wheldon)

of the Bosworth tunnel, 1,166 yards long but quite straight. The tunnel pierces hills which form a north-south watershed, between the Northamptonshire River Avon to the south and Leicestershire's principal river, the Soar, to the north.

The route of the railway has been following a line close to that of the canal but swerved slightly away to take a route through the lowest part of the hill, which it negotiated with a series of cuttings.

By following the path from the canal tunnel entrance, the one by which tow horses were led over the hill while boats were 'legged' through the tunnel, you will be able to see from the top of the hill the line of the shallow cutting of the railway. Descending the hill on the other side you can see clearly the bridge by which the A5199 road crosses the trackbed and, by following the canal path over the road, arrive at a point where it runs directly adjacent to the line for a short stretch. However, after diverging from the canal the trackbed here has disappeared into famland.

Now running in a north-easterly direction, and ignoring Husbands Bosworth for the reasons we have seen, the line had stations at Theddingworth and Lubenham before running into Market Harborough, crossing Farndon Road and Northampton Road. After the line was closed and the rails removed, the route became a popular dog-walking area. However, in the 1980s, the bridges over these roads were taken down and the line levelled to make way for housing. Rugby Close and Farndon Court are two of the new streets built where the line used to run.

The LNWR line from Market Harborough to Northampton is much easier to follow today, because for nearly all of its length it has been turned into a cycleway. The Brampton Valley Way is a 14-mile long cycleway and linear park running from Little Bowden Crossing in Market Harborough through rolling countryside to Boughton Crossing in Northamptonshire. It follows the trackbed of the disused railway, and includes two tunnels (cyclists need lights). The Way is situated mainly in Northamptonshire, for Market Harborough is only two miles from the county boundary. For further information, contact Station House, Lamport, Northampton, NN6 9HA.

The motive for building this line was the discovery in Northamptonshire of ironstone deposits, though the potential for passenger traffic was also a consideration. It opened on 16 February 1859. The line never attracted much in the way of passenger numbers, and intermediate stations between Market Harborough and Northampton started to close after the Second World War. Passenger services ended altogether on 4 January 1960. However, the Royal Train used the line as an overnight stopping place, near Lamport station, on several occasions.

As the ironstone workings in Northamptonshire declined, there was not even enough freight revenue to justify keeping the line open, and it formally closed on 16 August 1981. To mark the occasion, the previous day a final passenger train, a special four-coach diesel unit, ran between the two towns.

The Midland Railway had its own line between Leicester and Rugby, and this was even earlier than the LNWR Market Harborough to Rugby line. The Leicester to Rugby route was opened on 13 June 1840 by the Midland Counties Railway, one of the forerunners of the Midland Railway, but closed on 1 January 1962.

Running from Wigston North Junction (south of Leicester) to Rugby, the idea was to link Leicester to London via the London & Birmingham Railway. However,

Steps up to Crow Mill Way, a footpath recently created by the Blaby District Council using the embankment and trackbed of the old Midland Counties line. An informative explanation of the site and its history is on the interpretation board to the right of the picture. (Rodger Smith)

on 8 May 1857 it lost its status as a main line and simply became a branch line when the Midland Railway laid down its route to Hitchin (Midland trains then had running rights over Great Northern rails into London Kings Cross). The Hitchin arrangement in turn lasted until 1 October 1868 when the Midland Railway at last had a direct line into its own terminus, St Pancras.

Stations in Leicestershire were Wigston South, Countesthorpe, Broughton Astley, dating from 1840, and Ullesthorpe. Wigston South was just to the south of the big

118

triangular junction, which still today is one of the nodes of the railways in Leicestershire. The station was demolished (though still commemorated by a Station Street) and the area has been redeveloped. A bridlepath south from Blaby Road follows the line of the track, but ends at Countesthorpe Road.

However, just to the south here, at Crow Mill Bridge (589976), there is a car park and picnic site with an interpretation board erected by the Blaby District Council which tells you about the origins of the Midland Counties Railway. Crow Mill, an interesting building in its own right, is opposite. At this point a bridge viaduct (now demolished) took the railway over the valley containing the River Sence and the Grand Union Canal. The original bridge was built in 1840, and collapsed and was rebuilt, again in timber. There was another partial collapse in September 1852, due to excessive floodwater undermining the piers. It was again reconstructed in timber, but rebuilt in 1912 for the third and final time in masonry. It was demolished in 1984. The trackbed here has also recently been made

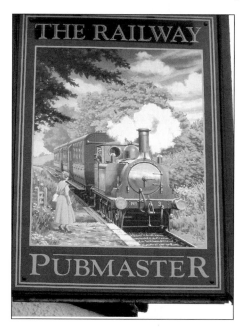

The attractive sign of the Railway Inn in Countesthorpe, a village which lost its railway and its station. (Rodger Smith)

The removal of a bridge at this point on Whetstone Gorse Lane has created one of the few gaps in the line of the trackbed, which is otherwise still surprisingly intact over the ten miles between Countesthorpe and Lillesthorpe. (Rodger Smith)

into a footpath, the Crow Mill Way (not marked on the OS map). Old railway sleepers have been used to edge some of the paths.

Countesthorpe still has a Railway Inn on Station Road, one of the village's principal roads. Though a large village (7,000 inhabitants) it now has no direct railway connections. The entrance to Penfold Drive, on the line of the old railway, leads to Linden Farm Drive, and off this road, on the left, is a footpath which brings you to a bridge over the old trackbed, the deep cutting of which is being used to grow Christmas trees.

At the OS map reference SP557935, a path crosses a field, giving access to an old bridge over the trackbed. The route of the line is severed here by the M1 motorway, itself running on a high embankment at this spot.

At Broughton Astley the coming of the railway brought an increase in the village's population. A local brickyard used the railway to carry away its bricks and roofing tiles. Almost every trace of the line has disappeared, though there is a remnant of embankment (securely fenced off) next to the car park of the Red Admiral public house (on yet another Station Road). In Victorian times the Red Admiral was known as the Station Hotel. The village also has a Station Farm. The bridge which carried the track over the road was demolished. South of the road a new housing estate occupies the route of the line.

At Leire there is a car park next to a playing field, indicated by a sign which says *Jubilee Walk Parking*. From here you can walk down to the old trackbed, which has been turned into a nature walk. The Leicestershire County Council, the Leire Parish Council, and local residents Mr and Mrs J.A. Redfern (whose donation made it possible) are to be thanked for this preservation effort. A hundred yards to the north the path stops at an embankment. You can climb steps to the top, and join the Leicestershire Round footpath, which goes off in a different direction. The line of the trackbed can just be made out as it disappears into fields. However, going south the Jubilee Way runs, at first through a steep cutting, to the Leire parish boundary, and a permissive path continues in the direction of Ullesthorpe. This permissive path extension seems to have been opened only very recently, a welcome sign that these old railway trackbeds are now being recognised as a wonderful recreational resource.

The Jubilee Walk has been created using the trackbed at Leire. The car park at the start of the path is close to this bridge on the road from Leire to Frolesworth. (Rodger Smith)

The last station on the line in Leicestershire was known as Ullesthorpe, or Ullesthorpe for Lutterworth. We saw in chapter 8 how, on the Market Harborough to Rugby line, the station at North Kilworth had to pretend to serve Lutterworth. The same thing happened at Ullesthorpe, five miles to the west of Lutterworth.

So the poor old town of Lutterworth, which for a century had been one of the most important posting stations on the London to Chester turnpike, found itself bypassed by both the Midland Railway and the LNWR. A horse-drawn omnibus service was set up to run from Lutterworth to

Ullesthorpe to connect with trains. It was not until the coming of the Great Central Railway at the end of the 19th century (see chapter 10) that Lutterworth had its own town railway station.

Ullesthorpe, however, had a cattle market, which made it an important station in its own right. On the corner of Mill Road is a village interpretation board, showing where the railway used to run. Mill Road passes a well-preserved windmill and leads to a footpath on to a golf course. The path, threading through the golf course, brings you alongside the old track bed, clearly visible at this point, in a line of trees. In the other direction, if you look from a bridge opposite the entrance to Mill Road, you will see (except in high summer when hidden by vegetation) the old station, now turned into an attractive private house, but with the down platform still visible in the garden. This house is reached by a street still bearing the name of Station Road, though new development has taken over some of the station site.

In 2005 John Poulter described a survey of the remains of the Leicester to Rugby line for the *Journal of the Railway and Canal Historical Society* (see Bibliography). This showed that 74% of the trackbed remained intact, 11% was occupied by buildings, and 10% (mainly cuttings) had been used for landfill and then returned to agriculture.

9
The Great Central Railway 1

Loughborough to Leicester

The frontage of the restored Loughborough Central station. (Rodger Smith)

The fastest, and the best – that was the proud boast of the Great Central Railway (GCR), one of the great railways of Britain. Once built, it certainly did provide the fastest route from Loughborough and Leicester to London. This made it a powerful competitor to the Midland Railway's own line to London. But while Midland Mainline expresses still thunder today through Leicestershire on the old Midland

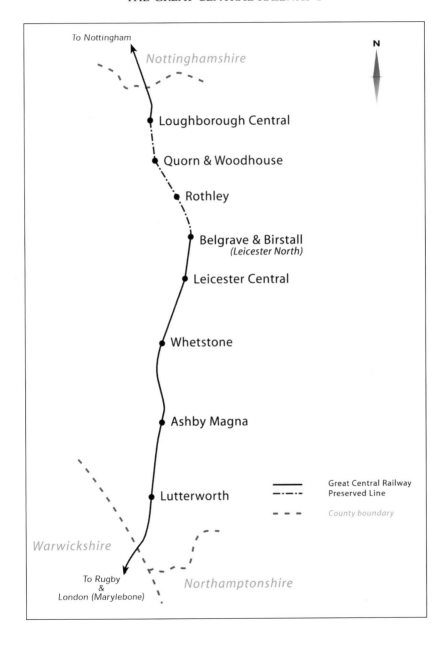

Railway route, in the 1960s British Rail ruthlessly chopped out the former GCR route from its network.

The Great Central Railway had been a hugely expensive undertaking, driven forward by the visionary zeal of Sir Edward Watkin. He was chairman of the Manchester, Sheffield and Lincolnshire Railway (MSLR). In 1893 he achieved his main goal, when Parliament approved his plan to link his lines in and around Sheffield with running rights over lines in the south to create a new main line to London. For this the railway would create its own London terminus, Marylebone. As soon as the approval was won the MSLR changed its name to Great Central Railway.

The GCR was the last main line ever planned in Britain, built with the confidence of men who thought that railways – as the only practical cross-country means of transport, whether for goods or people – were forever. They attached little importance, if they even knew about it, to the invention in 1884 in Germany of a propulsion device called the internal combustion engine.

Grades (i.e. climbs and descents) and curvature (i.e. bends) were kept to a minimum in the design, so as to facilitate optimum running at high speeds. This meant heavy expenditure on tunnels, cuttings and viaducts. The line was also built to the wider continental loading gauge, so that if the Channel Tunnel were ever built (Sir Edward Watkin was thinking big) the Great Central would be the one British railway to benefit from direct running to it and through it. It was also the first railway to adopt automatic colour light signalling. After 1923 the railway, now part of the LNER, used A3 Pacific locomotives designed by Sir Nigel Gresley, some of the finest steam locomotives ever built, on its top trains (such as the *Master Cutler* and the

South Yorkshireman) to compete with the LMS, which had taken over the Midland Railway.

The line had 60 years of glorious life, but nationalisation meant that Britain's railways became a single entity. The railway planners quickly reasoned that they had two parallel lines, the Midland and Great Central routes, in what they believed was wasteful competition with each other. One of them had to go, and the GCR was chosen to be sacrificed. So the Marylebone expresses, much favoured by Leicester businessmen, were withdrawn in 1961. Many of the intermediate stations on the line closed in 1963, after which passenger traffic was run down. Most freight ended in 1965. For some time a Nottingham to London 'semi-fast' service called at Leicester Central, but this could not compete with the expresses which ran via Leicester Midland and it, too, was withdrawn in 1966. All that was left then was a railcar service between Nottingham and Rugby, and that came to an end in 1969, after which the line was closed.

Running from north to south, the line entered Leicestershire from Nottinghamshire via the splendid 176-yard-long Stanford viaduct over the River Soar. The viaduct remains and there is still a railway line running over it. In fact, there is a continuous line from Ruddington in Nottinghamshire, which is sometimes used for test purposes. One mile south of the viaduct this has a connection to the south with the Midland line and the main rail network. But the old Great Central route into Loughborough was severed by the removal of an embankment. This route used to cross the Midland line, towards one end of the platforms at Loughborough Midland station, by a bridge. The bridge was demolished in 1980.

A GRC train on the line just north of Leicester. (Leicestershire Museums, Arts and Records Service)

The line then reached Loughborough Central station. This was built in 1899, but closed as a result of the Beeching cuts in 1969. After that date Loughborough, which once had three stations on the national railway network, was reduced to one, the station originally built by the Midland Railway. This is still on its original site off Nottingham Road and is as busy as ever with main line trains

But let us go back to re-tracing the lost Great Central line. To pick up the route again, we need to take the A60 road into Loughborough, and turn off into Great Central Road. We now arrive at the Loughborough Central station site.

The up platform of the restored Loughborough Central station, looking as neat and clean as at any time in its history. (Rodger Smith)

And as always in investigating lost railways we ask ourselves – what is there still to see? But here the answer is a surprising one: Everything.

Loughborough Central station has not only been preserved in its integrity, it has been refurbished and is immaculately maintained. For this is now the headquarters of the Great Central Railway (1976) plc, one of the country's most important heritage lines. The company was created to take over the assets of the Main Line Steam Trust, which had been formed in 1971 to try to save as much of the line as possible. Loughborough Central station became the northern terminus of an eight-mile section of preserved railway, where trains can pass each other on double tracks.

Loughborough Central station was reopened by this splendid company, mainly supported by volunteers, in 1974, only five years after closure. By then there had been considerable dilapidation caused by neglect and vandalism, but today the station is a delight. The entrance is on the road bridge, and you can see 'GCR 1898' on the gables made from Derbyshire gritstone. You enter a spacious booking hall, lined with varnished teak. Looking on to this is a neat little booking office. A wide fully canopied wooden staircase leads down to the station's island platform, which has a ridge and furrow canopy.

Great Central Railway (1976) plc now runs trains between Loughborough Central and Belgrave & Birstall (which has been re-christened Leicester North), with two intermediate stations. So the whole experience of the old Great Central (except the thunder of mighty expresses – speeds are limited by the rules of the Light Railway Order under which the line operates) can be savoured.

On the restored line, the 4.15 pm departing Loughborough Central for Quorn & Woodhouse, Rothley and Leicester North. (Rodger Smith)

Let us take one of the GCR trains. Out of Loughborough the scene quickly becomes rural. John Betjeman (1906-1984), the Poet Laureate, had in his earlier days written a poem on the Great Central Railway, and he enthused about this local stretch.

Above the fields of Leicestershire
On arches we were borne
And the rumble of the railway drowned
The thunder of the Quorn.

And, appropriately, the next station south of Loughborough is Quorn & Woodhouse (Quorn is also

132

sometimes known as Quorndon). In the mid-1920s, the heyday of the old Great Central line, Quorn & Woodhouse station could boast a stationmaster, a booking clerk, three porters, two signalmen, a ganger, and three or four platelayers, and, in winter, always a nice fire in the booking office. In the 1920s and 1930s the then Prince of Wales (later Edward VIII, and then the Duke of Windsor), being fond of hunting, often used the station before or after an outing with the Quorn. Sometimes he used the booking office as a changing room, while a porter posted outside kept the world at bay. The station was closed to passengers in 1963 and was then shorn of its canopies, but has now been restored to all its glory.

After Quorn the railway crosses the Swithland reservoir. At one time the GCR contemplated opening a station at Swithland to cater for 'excursionists' who might want to

Another of the afternoon's passenger trains on the restored railway arrives at Quorn & Woodhouse station. (Rodger Smith)

visit this attractive water feature in pleasant countryside, but a bricked-up arch in a bridge is now the only reminder.

Then we have Rothley station, built in 1899, closed in 1963, and reopened in 1976 (SK 568122). The station is entered down stairs from a road bridge, as at Loughborough Central. Rothley has an island platform, a glass canopy waiting area, and is lit by gas lamps, now carefully restored, the lamp standards being made of twisted iron.

David Ablitt, who walked the whole length of the line in the late 1960s, shortly after it closed, and has written an extensive unpublished memoir of his journey, had the good fortune to interview Madge Sleath, who had been a porter at Rothley during the First World War. In those days the first train of the day stopped at 5.56 am and the last at 10.50 pm. Madge worked six 12-hour shifts and alternate Sundays, a 72-hour week, for which she received 19 shillings. On one occasion, in a pause between helping load and unload coal carts, she picked up a bit of rope and started skipping. Some officious railway high-up must have seen her from a passing train, because a telegraph message was sent to the stationmaster: 'Female porter seen skipping in goods yard stop had she nothing better to do stop'. When she heard about the revival of the line, Madge Sleath volunteered her services and took a job in the refreshment rooms, retiring only in 1980, at the age of 84.

In the days when this was part of the national rail network there was a Leicester suburban station called Belgrave & Birstall. This is now the southernmost part of the restored heritage line, and has been rechristened Leicester North. A new station has been constructed on the site of the old one, which had been badly vandalised. The first train to Leicester North on the revived railway ran on 3 July 1991.

MADGE CAMP
FEMALE PORTER 1915-1919

Madge Sleath (née Camp), a female porter at Rothley. (Great Central Heritage Railway)

South from Leicester North there are only relics of the railway, which once ran through the centre of the city on a great viaduct, with its 97 arches in traditional railway blue brick. This viaduct (together with girder bridges over roads) ran for 35 chains (more than a mile) across the centre of Leicester, giving wonderful views over the city. To enable it to be built, some 250 houses had to be demolished, and the residents re-housed at the railway's expense. Some streets, such as the old Sycamore Lane, disappeared altogether.

Most of this wonderful viaduct has now gone, as have the bridges across intersecting roads. In some places, truncated pieces of the viaduct can be seen, the arches underneath often used as workshops. One is in Ravensbridge Drive, and there is a longer section (with eleven arches) off Slater Street. Between these two a girder bridge over the River Soar was demolished and removed for scrap in the 1980s. Precise descriptions of every remaining relic (bridge abutments, pieces of embankment) can be found on the enthusiasts' website www.gcrleicester.info.

10
The Great Central Railway 2

Leicester to Lutterworth

The platform indicator at Leicester Central Station, in its glory days at the beginning of the 20th century. (Leicestershire Museums, Arts and Records Service)

Leicester Central station was built high above the city, on a continuation of that massive Great Central Railway viaduct coming in from the north.

The actual location of the station was between Northgate Street and Bath Street, with All Saints Road passing underneath (abutments can still be seen in this road). A bowstring girder bridge took the viaduct over Northgate

Leicester Central station shortly before demolition. (Leicestershire Museums, Arts and Records Service)

Street, and it then widened out until it was 190 ft wide at this point. The base of the station was in Staffordshire Blue bricks, a favourite with railway builders.

Leicester Central, in common with most GCR stations, had a single island platform. This was 1,300 ft long and 85 ft wide in the middle, though slightly tapering, and had two bays at either end for local services. These bays were themselves 430 ft long. A canopy stretched 830 ft along the platform. Entrance was from street level, from Jarvis Street or Great Central Street.

The southern end of the station crossed the old Jewry Wall Street. Here the railway construction work uncovered, in a cellar, the Blackfriars Roman pavement,

The east frontage of Leicester Central station today, shorn of its gables and used for car repairs and by a car wash firm. (Rodger Smith)

with a mosaic. The railway company was asked to build a special chamber to protect it. A thick glass panel allowed the mosaic, the ownership of which was retained by the Leicester Corporation, to be viewed from the platform above. In 1976 it was removed to the Jewry Wall Museum.

The façade of the station in Great Central Street was in red brick and terracotta, and there was a clock tower. On one side of the façade was the vehicle entrance for the parcels offices, with wrought-iron gates, and a tile frieze that read 'Great Central Railway'. The waiting area for taxis, behind the façade, had a glass roof. The booking hall was at ground level, and stairs led up to the platforms.

The old GCR parcels office pediment is still intact. (Rodger Smith)

But part of the old station area itself, at a higher level, is occupied by modern industrial units and (to the south of this picture) an open-air car park. (Rodger Smith)

The upper station buildings are now put to industrial use. But even in a dilapidated state they show the attractive gables and ornamentation which once also adorned the frontage. (Judy Wheldon)

There was a large hydraulic lift for luggage. The Great Central's refreshment room had brown and green vitrified tiles with railway wheel motif, with dark woodwork. The kitchen was beneath the platform. When it closed on 29 December 1951, nearly 30 years after the Great Central had become part of the LNER, this refreshment room still had original fittings as well as plates, cutlery and crockery with the arms of the Great Central.

Because Leicester was the halfway point for GCR trains running between Manchester and London, locomotives were often changed there, and so to the south of the station

The Blackfriars Roman mosaic, uncovered by work on the Great Central Railway. After being preserved by the railway authorities for 75 years, it was moved in 1976 to Leicester's Jewry Wall Museum, where it can now be viewed. (Judy Wheldon)

there was a large locomotive shed and goods facilities. The shed could hold 20 steam locomotives and employed a staff of about 70. At the corner of Soar Lane and Northgate Street was the Great Central Hotel.

After withdrawal of London through trains on 3 September 1966, Leicester Central became an unstaffed halt served by Rugby to Nottingham stopping trains made up of railcars. The very last train from the station departed 3 May 1969, witnessed by a large crowd.

After that the station was locked up, and the tracks were lifted. The station was used to store scrap metal, and the

The viaduct that carried the Great Central Railway, seen from the west. (Rodger Smith)

arches at ground level were let out as small industrial units. The platform buildings, canopies and platforms themselves were bulldozed down in 1970. Steadily, the old GCR viaduct through Leicester was removed to allow for road improvements or industrial development. The huge bowstring bridge at Northgate Street went in 1981.The Great Central Hotel was also demolished and the site developed.

At ground level, however, the station brick and terracotta façade is mostly intact, except for the gables (removed in BR days). The gates are still in position, though looking a little rickety. The station area is now used for car repairs and a car wash. The bridge over All Saints Road is still in situ, giving a good impression of the width of the area occupied by the station. The Parcels Office entrance with its tile frieze is the most prominent survivor of GCR days. The letters GCR are still there in terracotta above the parcels bay entrance. The viaduct arches on Jarvis Street are still being used by small industrial units. Where Jarvis Street becomes Blackfriars Street there is a larger archway, once the entrance to the booking hall. At the higher level there is an extensive car park, and some industrial units.

The future of the station area is not clear. One possibility would be to demolish the viaduct on which the station stood, in order to uncover the archaeological remains of the old Roman city. Another possibility is that, with the arches, the site would be regenerated with bars, restaurants and flats, adjacent to a new large marina area leading off the River Soar.

From the end of Leicester Central station, the viaduct continued for another 28½ chains to span Welles Street, Bath Lane, the River Soar at the junction of St Augustine Street and West Bridge Street, and an old course of the River Soar, where the viaduct ended. As the line of the railway came down closer to ground level, it became easier to preserve the route.

And now commuters still come into the centre of Leicester using the old Great Central Railway. But this time, the commuters are cyclists. They use a cycle path (also available for horse-riding and as a footpath), called Great Central Way, laid along the course of the old line. In the morning they come streaming into the centre, and in the evening the stream goes in the other direction. To the south of the city Great Central Way becomes Whetstone Way, then Bramble Way.

Different parts of the Great Central Way today are owned by the Leicester City Council, the Leicestershire County Council, the Blaby District Council and the Glen Parva Parish Council. In the Leicester City section there is at present a magnificent surviving bowstring bridge, whose fate is uncertain.

South of the bridge, Great Central Way path follows a level, straight course to the outskirts of the city. As we come out of the city the line and modern path cross the Soar Valley and the Grand Union Canal on another superb bridge at Aylestone.

The line now starts to run parallel with the Grand Union Canal and the River Soar. The Great Central Way,

The threatened bowstring bridge that the authorities want to demolish. (Judy Wheldon)

continuing on its way south, has some attractive paths running from it, particularly into woods at Glen Parva and the Glen Parva nature reserve. It comes to an abrupt end at a point where the trackbed has been taken into fields, and traces of it have disappeared. The cycleway turns left and continues as the Gurlaxton Way.

Turning right, a footpath brings you to the Grand Union Canal, which you cross at Gee's Lock. Walking south along the canal towpath, which makes a right-angle bend, you come to the abutments of the old GCR bridge. Here you can climb back up to the track and walk a short distance

The bridge (in the background) at Aylestone that used to carry the Great Central line over canal and river, and now carries the Great Central cycleway. (Judy Wheldon)

Part of the Great Central Way cycle path that follows the old GCR trackbed. (Rodger Smith)

south, before being brought up sharply at a corrugated iron fence.

The trackbed recrosses the River Sence by a girder bridge. Whetstone had its own station, and still has a Station Road, though the site of the station is now covered by Spinney Halt Estate.

The track then climbed to the next station at Ashby Magna, which survived till the bitter end. It was a typical GCR station, accessed from a road bridge. The line took a sharp curve, known as 'Cosby Corner', near Whetstone and Cosby. At Gilmorton Road, near Ashby Magna, the sides of a bridge are intact, though the trackbed here, running on an embankment, is heavily overgrown.

Here and for the next 5½ miles, running alongside the route of the old Great Central, is a more modern transport artery, the M1 motorway. You have to be sharp-eyed (and a passenger not a driver!) to see the traces of the GCR from the motorway today, but by coming off the M1 at Junction 20, taking the direction of Lutterworth, and turning left at the roundabout (a model of an early jet plane – made in Lutterworth - stands in the middle of the roundabout) onto the A426 in the direction of Rugby, and then taking the first left (Swinford Lane), you will come across the trackbed running south towards Warwickshire.

The view of the trackbed looking south from Swinford Lane, Lutterworth. (Rodger Smith)

Lutterworth station. (Leicestershire Museums, Arts and Records Service)

On the other side of the M1, however, the embankment is very overgrown. The trackbed disappears for a short stretch in Lutterworth itself.

Lutterworth station was the most southerly in the county. By the time the GCR was built, Lutterworth was the largest town in Leicestershire without its own station, so the coming of the GCR was warmly welcomed. It was recorded that a local character called 'Jesus' Drake bought the first ticket. The station was situated in Ely Road, which was renamed Station Road.

And so the line ran south through Warwickshire to its final destination, Marylebone station in London. The old prestigious GCR hotel at Marylebone, which became offices, has recently been reopened and refurbished as a luxury hotel.

Conclusion

The age of the train is certainly not over, and enthusiasts are coming up with all sorts of revival schemes. One particularly concerns Leicestershire. Sir Edward Watkin's vision of a direct line from the Midlands to the Continent is being re-imagined. The Central Railway Company has been formed to try to recreate a line from Rugby to the Channel Tunnel. From Rugby they would bring a new route up to the east of Countesthorpe to meet the existing railway network at Wigston Junction.

But the purpose of this book is not to speculate on the future of railways, or what this century may bring in the realm of public transport. The *Lost Railways* series of books aims to record what passenger railways now no longer in operation were like when they were in their heyday, and to trace what remains today. And when you go to look, it is surprising how many of the old routes can still be traced on the ground because, in the 19th century, railway construction work, whether embankments or cuttings, tunnels or bridges, was all built to last. The Victorians thought railways were the future, and might last for centuries. The poet Tennyson once wrote: 'Let the great world spin for ever down the ringing grooves of change'. (As an aside we should mention that Tennyson might have been a great poet, but he was not a practical man if he thought that railway trains ran in grooves!)

As the campaign to save the bowstring bridge in the centre of Leicester, or the enthusiastic crowds who go to

Loughborough to enjoy the revived Great Central Railway have shown, there is now a great deal of enthusiasm for preserving the best of Victorian railway engineering.

And Leicestershire and Rutland can boast some of the finest examples in the country, from the great viaducts – Harringworth or Marefield – to the humblest village station.

Bibliography

Ablitt, David, *A Walk along the Great Central Railway*, unpublished manuscript.

Anderson, P. Howard, *Forgotten Railways, Volume 2 – The East Midlands*, 2nd edition, David & Charles, 1985.

Biddle, Gordon, *Britain's Historic Railway Buildings*, Oxford University Press, 2003.

Birt, David, 'Wilson Station, an Early Closure', in *Midland Railway Society Journal*, issue 28, summer 2005.

Carr, Louie, *Working the Bluebell Line*, reprint, Loughborough [the story of fireman Harry Preston].

Clinker, C.R., *Leicester and Swannington Railway*, Avon.

Dank, Malcolm, *A History of the Charnwood Forest Railway*, reprint, Loughborough.

Davies, Hunter, *George Stephenson*, Sutton Publishing Ltd, 2004.

Duffell, Stephen, 'Clement E. Stretton, Railway Engineer, Historian and Collector', *Journal of the Railway & Canal Historical Society*, vol. 35, part 3, no. 193, November 2005 [Clement Stretton was the leading early historian of Leicestershire railways].

Ellis, Hamilton, *The Midland Railway*, Ian Allan Ltd, 1953.

Franks, D.L., *Great Northern and London & North-Western Joint Railway*.

Gamble, Horace A., *Railways around Leicester*, Anderson Publications, 1989.

Gough, John, *Northampton and Harborough Line*, RCHS, 1989.

Hawkins, Mac, *The Great Central, Then and Now*, BCA, 1992.

Healy, John M.C., *The last days of steam in Leicestershire and Rutland*, Alan Sutton, 1989.

Helsey, M., *A history of the Charnwood Forest Railway*, reprint, Loughborough.

Henshaw, Alfred, *The Great Northern Railway in the East Midlands*, Railway Correspondence Society 2002.

Jacques, John C., *Railway Tales, Nostalgic Stories from the Age of Steam*.

Lee, Charles E., *Swannington: one-time railway centre*, article first published in *Railway Magazine*, facsimile reprinted by Swannington Heritage Trust.

Leicestershire County Council Libraries and Information Service, *Images of Loughborough*, Breedon Books Publishing.

Moore, Andrew, *Leicestershire's Stations, Historic Postcards*. Laurel House Publishing.

Moore, Andrew, *Leicestershire's Stations, an Historical Perspective*, Laurel House Publishing, 1998.

Morton, Richard, 'Manton', *Midland Railway Society Journal*, issue no. 25.

Poulter, John, 'Linear Legacies, the disappearance of closed transport routes, as illustrated by the Midland Counties railway line between Rugby and Leicester', in *Journal of the Railway & Canal Historical Society*, vol. 35 part 2 no. 192, July 2005.

Rolt, L.T.C., *The Making of a Railway*, Hugh Evelyn Ltd, 1971.

Stratton, Clement E., *Notes on the Leicester and Swannington Railway*, 1891 lecture notes, published by the Swannington Heritage Trust.

Stretton, John, *British Railways Past and Present – Leicestershire*, Past & Present Publishing Ltd, 2004.

Stretton, John, *Leicestershire Railway Memories*, Unicorn Books, 1989.

Walker, Colin, *Great Central Twilight*, Pendyke Publications, 2000.

Welbourn, Nigel, *Lost lines – LMR*, Ian Allan Publishing, 1994.

White, Peter M., *Burton & Ashby Tramways*, Middleton Press, 2000.

Williams, Roy, *The Midland Railway, A New History*, David & Charles, 1988.

Websites

www.battlefield-line-railway.co.uk (Nuneaton to Ashby line, preserved section)

www.meltonmowbray.steamrailways.com (Bottesford to Hallaton line)

www.nottm-melton-railway.co.uk (Nottingham to Kettering line)

www.railwayarchive.org.uk (Great Central Railway)

www.swannington-heritage.co.uk (Leicester to Swannington line)

www.ukhrail.uel.ac (Rutland Railway Museum)

Index